To Squelch
from ————— Rose
Xmas 1987

D0513804

THE WINNING EDGE

THE WINNING EDGE

Jeremy Flint

faber and faber

LONDON · BOSTON

First published in 1986 by
Faber and Faber Limited
3 Queen Square London WC1N 3AU

Phototypeset by Wilmaset Birkenhead Wirral
Printed in Great Britain by
Redwood Burn Ltd Trowbridge Wiltshire
All rights reserved

Foreword © Irving Rose 1986
Text © Jeremy Flint 1986

The author is grateful to the editor of the *The Times* for permission to reproduce material from his weekly articles.

British Library Cataloguing in Publication Data
Flint, Jeremy
The winning edge.
1. Contract bridge
I. Title
795.41′5   GV1282.3
ISBN 0–571–14738–0
ISBN 0–571–14536–1 Pbk

Library of Congress Cataloging-in-Publication Data
Flint, Jeremy, 1928–
The winning edge.
1. Contract bridge.   I. Title.
GV1282.3.F545   1986   795.41′53   86–13388
ISBN 0–571–14738–0
ISBN 0–571–14536–1 (pbk.)

CONTENTS

FOREWORD

by Irving Rose

It was raining cats and dogs the first time I went to Jeremy Flint's little Chelsea house in 1967, which provided a good excuse for staying the night. My interest wasn't bridge, but Jeremy's stepdaughter Annette, who was later to become my wife.

That night became a week, a month, a year. And then we moved to a large flat in the Old Brompton Road where, despite the occasional squabble, the Flints and the Roses lived happily for twelve years.

Inevitably, I suppose, Jeremy and I formed a bridge partnership. We are totally different in our approach to the game. Jeremy is systematic, logical, and always searching for the extra chance; I don't like rigid systems and much prefer to play a more buccaneering game. I rely on flair and speed, which I believe score a handsome profit on balance, even if I have to put up with a few scowls from across the table.

In *The Winning Edge* Jeremy sets out the various considerations that influence an expert to take a marginal decision. It reminds me of the days we played together. There are many memories, but the incident which reveals the way his mind works had nothing to do with bridge.

The four of us had gone to Hong Kong where Jeremy was commentating on the Far Eastern Championships. After we had played in the Pairs Championship, which we won, there was a free day. We thought we'd celebrate by going to Macao by hydrofoil. Jeremy rarely plays casino games, but on this occasion he agreed to become partners at Punto Banco. It is a silly game, I admit, where the house has an advantage you can't beat. However, Jeremy spotted a Chinaman who seemed to be having a disastrous run. 'Rose,' he said, 'when this one goes Banco, you go Punto, and vice versa.'

For nine successive hands the 'system' won. Jeremy left the table for a moment and returned, pleased to see the Chinaman lose the tenth coup. His pleasure was short-lived. 'I'm afraid I bet on the same side as the Chinaman,' I confessed. 'I felt sorry for him.'

Jeremy looked at me as if I had passed him in a cue bid.

1

Obstacle-race with a steeplechaser

It was twenty to eleven when Irving Rose rang the doorbell. 'I thought we said 10 o'clock,' I said. 'Tennish,' Rose replied with no sign of contrition.

The next few minutes were spent in the discussion of our system, an indispensable prelude to any Gold Cup match. But it was not long before he changed the subject to matters dearer to his heart. In some ways Rose's bidding reminds me of a steeplechaser whose brilliant speed is marred by reckless disregard of the obstacles.

The match had only just started when Rose cantered towards the first ditch:

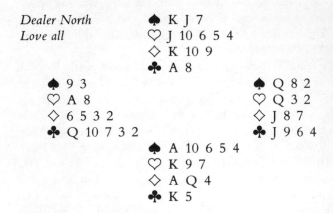

Dealer North
Love all

♠ K J 7
♡ J 10 6 5 4
♢ K 10 9
♣ A 8

♠ 9 3
♡ A 8
♢ 6 5 3 2
♣ Q 10 7 3 2

♠ Q 8 2
♡ Q 3 2
♢ J 8 7
♣ J 9 6 4

♠ A 10 6 5 4
♡ K 9 7
♢ A Q 4
♣ K 5

It looks like an uneventful 3NT or four hearts or four spades, doesn't it? Oh no!

South	West	North	East
Rose		Flint	
—	—	1♡	No
1♠	No	1NT	No
2♣[1]	No	2♠	No
3◇	No	4♠	No
4NT[2]	No	5◇	No
6♠	No	No	No

[1] My 1NT rebid had a wide range and two clubs was a form of enquiry.

[2] As my bidding had shown a minimum opening with three spades, and I had not made any slam try over three diamonds, this was wholly unjustified. The conventional gadget, as so often happens, has obscured a simple problem of valuation.

Rose received the lead of the ace of hearts, which did him no harm, followed by a club switch. A losing spade finesse brought the proceedings to a mercifully swift conclusion. Rose lit a cigarette, pointedly ignoring my raised eyebrow.

We usually avoid any kind of discussion until after the play, but I had to know. 'Why did you play against the odds?' I asked. 'If West has the singleton 8 or 9 of spades you can succeed against a 4–1 break, can't you?' 'Of course,' he answered. 'But (a) his lead of the ace of hearts might have meant that he had something like Q x x of trumps; and (b) I played the first spade from hand, if you remember; if the 8 or 9 had appeared I might have reconsidered.'

An interesting point arises from this: if in the West position you hold something like Q 9 x or Q 8 x in front of dummy's K J x, it may be good play to insert the 8 or 9.

At half-time in this match our team trailed by 30 IMPs.

Like a family temporarily embarrassed by a whiff of
scandal, we preserved an insouciant united front. This was
a successful, if lucky, counter-punch:

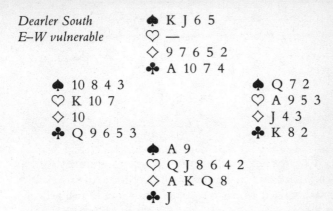

Dearler South
E–W vulnerable

♠ K J 6 5
♥ —
♦ 9 7 6 5 2
♣ A 10 7 4

♠ 10 8 4 3
♥ K 10 7
♦ 10
♣ Q 9 6 5 3

♠ Q 7 2
♥ A 9 5 3
♦ J 4 3
♣ K 8 2

♠ A 9
♥ Q J 8 6 4 2
♦ A K Q 8
♣ J

To avoid any risk of outraging Mrs Whitehouse,
upholder of decency, I will not describe the bidding. The
final contract was six diamonds by South, and West led a
friendly 3 of spades, which ran to the queen and ace.

If you work it out, you will find that there is a sound
play for this contract if the trumps are 2–2 and the hearts
4–3. Declarer ruffed a heart in dummy and returned to the
♦ Q, noting West's ♦ 10 with interest. A second heart
ruff was followed by the king and jack of spades. South
would have been happy to see East ruff, but East followed.
After some cross-ruffing in clubs and hearts South reached
this end position:

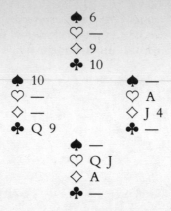

   As the cards lie, South can ruff a heart in dummy for his eleventh trick and make the twelfth with the ♢ A. But if West had started with ♢ J 10, declarer would still prevail. West would ruff the heart, but South would make the last two tricks.

   After some anxious moments we won the match by 11 IMPs.

2

Suicide, fratricide and family contracts

In a normal 'suicide' squeeze one defender is squeezed by his partner. The *Official Encyclopaedia of Bridge* points out that the nomenclature seems faulty and goes on to suggest that the play should be called a 'cannibal' squeeze. But that isn't quite right either, because in the jungle it is the visitor who goes into the pot, not a fellow member of the tribe. So perhaps the 'fratricide' squeeze would give a better picture.

Two instructive examples of the coup appeared in a bulletin of the International Bridge Press Association, the first from a match between Italy and Israel.

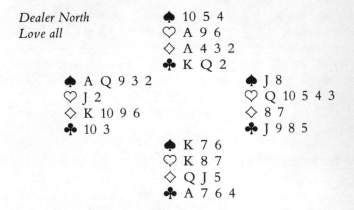

Dealer North
Love all

	♠ 10 5 4	
	♡ A 9 6	
	◇ A 4 3 2	
	♣ K Q 2	
♠ A Q 9 3 2		♠ J 8
♡ J 2		♡ Q 10 5 4 3
◇ K 10 9 6		◇ 8 7
♣ 10 3		♣ J 9 8 5
	♠ K 7 6	
	♡ K 8 7	
	◇ Q J 5	
	♣ A 7 6 4	

South was in 3NT and Franco, sitting West for Italy, led the 2 of spades. (Third and fifth best leads have in many countries superseded the old fourth best.) The declarer, Levit, headed the jack of spades with the king and

advanced the jack of diamonds. This was covered by the
king and ace. South could count eight tricks now, with the
possibility of a ninth from a 3–3 break in either diamonds
or clubs. What do you suppose he did next?

Correct, he exited with a spade. He reckoned that if
West played off four spade winners some squeeze would
develop. So it would have done, but West was too wily.
He cashed just three tricks in spades, East discarding two
hearts, then switched to the jack of hearts. Now it was
impossible for the declarer to exert any pressure and he
finished one down.

Quite often the defenders have no answer to a suicide
(or fratricide) squeeze. The declarer on this occasion was a
Hungarian international.

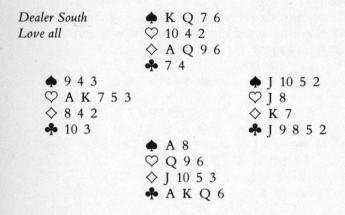

Dealer South
Love all

		♠ K Q 7 6	
		♡ 10 4 2	
		◇ A Q 9 6	
		♣ 7 4	

♠ 9 4 3		♠ J 10 5 2
♡ A K 7 5 3		♡ J 8
◇ 8 4 2		◇ K 7
♣ 10 3		♣ J 9 8 5 2

	♠ A 8	
	♡ Q 9 6	
	◇ J 10 5 3	
	♣ A K Q 6	

The bidding went:

South	West	North	East
1♣	No	1♠	No
2NT	No	3NT	No
No	No		

West led a low heart to the jack and queen. South promptly returned a heart. This, as you see, was very effective. If West plays all his hearts his partner is squeezed, and if West switches after making just three winners, then the declarer can afford to give up a diamond. Note that South could assume from the first that the diamond finesse would be wrong, because West with five hearts to the A K and the ◇ K would have overcalled at the one level.

A genuine suicide squeeze, in which a defender damages himself rather than his partner, is rare, but it can happen. Study this deal:

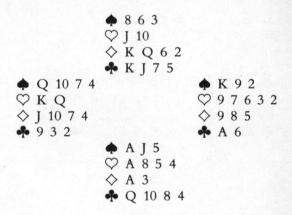

```
                ♠ 8 6 3
                ♡ J 10
                ◇ K Q 6 2
                ♣ K J 7 5
  ♠ Q 10 7 4                  ♠ K 9 2
  ♡ K Q                       ♡ 9 7 6 3 2
  ◇ J 10 7 4                  ◇ 9 8 5
  ♣ 9 3 2                     ♣ A 6
                ♠ A J 5
                ♡ A 8 5 4
                ◇ A 3
                ♣ Q 10 8 4
```

West leads a low spade against 3NT and the king loses to the ace. East wins the first club and returns the 9 of spades. If West takes three spade tricks, giving the defenders their book of four tricks, then West will later be squeezed by the fourth club and South will make the contract. Instead of cashing the long spade, West must exit with the king of hearts. Now he can discard the spade winner on the fourth club and South will have nowhere to go for his ninth trick.

3

Early indication of a dead duck

It is strange how reluctant most bridge players are to accept the blame, isn't it? The following hand stayed in my mind because East drew attention to a small mistake of his own that no one else at the table had even considered.

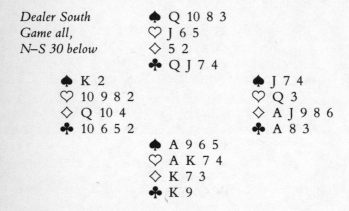

Dealer South
Game all,
N–S 30 below

♠ Q 10 8 3
♡ J 6 5
◇ 5 2
♣ Q J 7 4

♠ K 2
♡ 10 9 8 2
◇ Q 10 4
♣ 10 6 5 2

♠ J 7 4
♡ Q 3
◇ A J 9 8 6
♣ A 8 3

♠ A 9 6 5
♡ A K 7 4
◇ K 7 3
♣ K 9

South opened 1NT and North, at 30 up, raised to 2NT. This was quite sensible, I think, though on the combined hands three spades might have been a better contract.

West led the 9 of hearts against 2NT, indicating a combination headed by 10 9. The 9 ran to South's king and the declarer's first move was to play ace and another spade. West pressed on with the 8 of hearts and East's queen was taken by the ace. South now cleared his tricks in clubs and when East led a diamond South's king held the trick.

'I'm sorry,' said West, 'I suppose we can beat it if I switch to a diamond after the king of spades.'

Most players in East's position would have grunted agreement, but East spoke up rather unexpectedly. 'I don't think you could tell,' he said. 'I could have helped you by playing the queen of hearts on the first round. I knew it was a dead duck.'

Quite true, and there was something else that East might have done. Suppose on the second round of spades he had dropped the *jack*. This would have been a variation of the Smith convention: an unnatural card asking partner not to do the obvious thing. Another name for this type of play is 'the Oddball'.

The events on the next hand were of a more familiar kind.

Dealer South   ♠ A 10 9 6 4
Love all   ♡ J 9 8 6
                    ♢ 7 2
                    ♣ 8 4

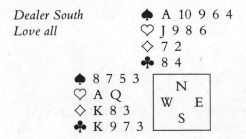

♠ 8 7 5 3
♡ A Q
♢ K 8 3
♣ K 9 7 3

A player buttonholed me in the bar. 'Here's a hand you might like to use in one of your articles,' he began. 'South plays in four hearts after a simple one heart – two hearts – four hearts. You lead a spade. Declarer takes the ace and discards the jack of clubs from hand. Then he runs the jack of hearts, which you win with the queen. What do you do now?'

Well, I'm not absolutely green. To justify his bidding, South must be 5–5 in the red suits, or something like that. The danger was that he would establish his diamonds and discard a club from dummy.

'I dare say you can afford to play another spade for the moment,' I said. 'But probably you should attack the clubs at once.'

'You're not afraid that he might have A Q J of clubs?'

'Hardly; in that case he would have discarded a diamond and finessed the club at trick two.'

'Yes, I suppose so. Anyway, I did lead a club and we beat the contract.' He proudly showed me the full hand:

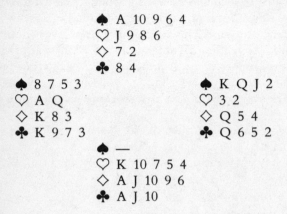

```
                ♠ A 10 9 6 4
                ♡ J 9 8 6
                ◇ 7 2
                ♣ 8 4
♠ 8 7 5 3                       ♠ K Q J 2
♡ A Q                           ♡ 3 2
◇ K 8 3                         ◇ Q 5 4
♣ K 9 7 3                       ♣ Q 6 5 2
                ♠ —
                ♡ K 10 7 5 4
                ◇ A J 10 9 6
                ♣ A J 10
```

A day or two later somebody else showed me the same hand. He was South and his story was that the defence didn't play a club at any point.

4

Harsh blow from an unexpected quarter

Players quite often say, 'I had a blind spot.' As a rule, it's not true; they have just been incompetent and would probably do the same thing again in the same circumstances. Occasionally a tournament player will do something quite ridiculous; it happened in the semifinal of the 1984 Olympiad when a Polish player, on the very last board, made two extraordinary mistakes, but this was due to nerves rather than to blindness. So, what should one say about the good player who muddled the following deal?

```
Dealer North            ♠ A 7
Neither vulnerable,     ♡ J 4
N–S 60 below            ◇ K 10 8 3
                        ♣ A K Q 9 4

♠ K J 8 3 2                          ♠ 10 9 4
♡ K Q 9 7 2                          ♡ 6 3
◇ 7                                  ◇ J 6 5 4
♣ 10 8                               ♣ J 6 5 2

                        ♠ Q 6 5
                        ♡ A 10 8 5
                        ◇ A Q 9 2
                        ♣ 7 3
```

South	West	North	East
—	—	1♣	No
1◇	1♠	3◇	No
3♡	No	3♠	No
4◇	No	5♣	No
5◇	No	No	No

After flirting with the diamond slam, North–South stopped on the verge.

West led the king of hearts. South won and played ace and king of diamonds, discovering the 4–1 break. Then he exited with the jack of hearts to West's queen; this was good play, because it would not help the defence to play a third round of hearts, forcing East to ruff. Realizing this, West led a club. South cashed the top clubs, discarding a spade from hand, then finessed the diamond 9. This left:

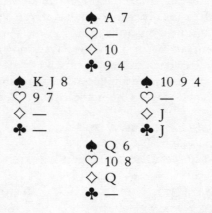

```
                 ♠ A 7
                 ♡ —
                 ◇ 10
                 ♣ 9 4
   ♠ K J 8                   ♠ 10 9 4
   ♡ 9 7                     ♡ —
   ◇ —                       ◇ J
   ♣ —                       ♣ J
                 ♠ Q 6
                 ♡ 10 8
                 ◇ Q
                 ♣ —
```

South led the 10 of hearts and discarded a spade from dummy. He had a clear idea what would happen: East would ruff and lead a spade; then a club ruff and dummy would be high.

But East, normally no great striker of the ball, realized that the contract would be made if he ruffed the heart, so he discarded a spade. South shrugged and ruffed his last heart. Now East overruffed and played a spade, leaving South a trick short.

Admittedly, East's refusal to ruff was a harsh blow from an unexpected quarter. Still, South knew the position. A spade to the ace, a club ruff and a spade ruff would have safely provided three of the last four tricks, which was all that South required. Blind spot? No, just careless play.

The declarer on the next deal was a less talented performer. This did not stop him from dogmatically insisting that his contract was impossible to make.

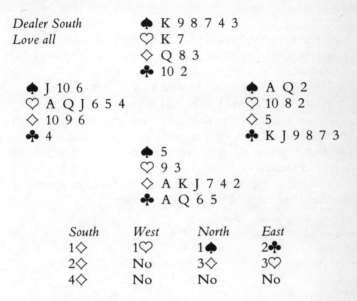

Dealer South
Love all

```
                    ♠ K 9 8 7 4 3
                    ♡ K 7
                    ◇ Q 8 3
                    ♣ 10 2
♠ J 10 6                              ♠ A Q 2
♡ A Q J 6 5 4                         ♡ 10 8 2
◇ 10 9 6                              ◇ 5
♣ 4                                   ♣ K J 9 8 7 3
                    ♠ 5
                    ♡ 9 3
                    ◇ A K J 7 4 2
                    ♣ A Q 6 5
```

South	West	North	East
1◇	1♡	1♠	2♣
2◇	No	3◇	3♡
4◇	No	No	No

West led his singleton club, dummy played low, and East the jack. South won and led a heart; West played the ace and made the good return of a low trump. Now South led the ace of clubs. West ruffed and played another diamond; this left the declarer with two losing clubs and only one trump in dummy, so he lost in the end a spade, a heart, a ruff and the fourth club.

The safe line here was to play a low club at trick two, not risking the ace. The other low club can be ruffed with the queen of trumps if necessary, and there will be ten tricks on top.

5

Simplicity masks a plan of brilliance

The redoubtable Pakistani, Zia Mahmood, was back in England after a tour that had taken him to Monte Carlo, Pakistan and New York.

'How did you get on?' I asked him.

'All right. We won the Reisinger in New York.'

This is one of the two most prestigious team events in America. One of his team-mates was Matt Granovetter, who had made a big impression in one of the British television series.

'Let me show you a couple of hands,' Zia went on, reaching for the inevitable scrap of paper.

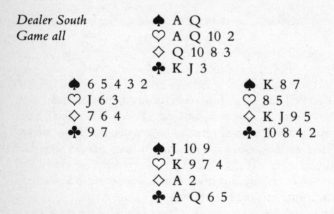

Dealer South
Game all

	♠ A Q	
	♡ A Q 10 2	
	◇ Q 10 8 3	
	♣ K J 3	
♠ 6 5 4 3 2		♠ K 8 7
♡ J 6 3		♡ 8 5
◇ 7 6 4		◇ K J 9 5
♣ 9 7		♣ 10 8 4 2
	♠ J 10 9	
	♡ K 9 7 4	
	◇ A 2	
	♣ A Q 6 5	

Zia, South, became declarer in six hearts. West led the 7 of diamonds, which was covered by the 8, 9 and ace.

When the trumps break 3–2 there are eleven sure tricks in sight. It may seem that a simple way to arrive at a twelfth would be to draw trumps, cash the clubs, then lead a diamond to the 10 and jack, forcing East to set up a trick either for the queen of spades or the queen of diamonds.

There is a slight drawback to this plan, which most players would overlook. All would be well if East had only three clubs, but if he had four, then what would dummy throw on the fourth round of clubs?

Zia foresaw this problem and solved it in an unusual way. When in dummy after the third round of trumps he cashed the ace of spades, then played four rounds of clubs, discarding dummy's queen of spades. This left:

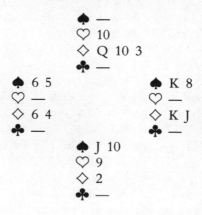

The 2 of diamonds ran to the jack, and East was end-played. It would have made no difference, obviously, if West had held the king of spades.

This was Zia's second hand:

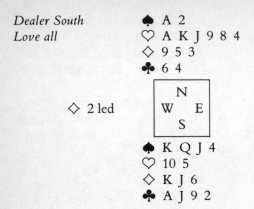

Dealer South
Love all

♠ A 2
♡ A K J 9 8 4
♢ 9 5 3
♣ 6 4

◇ 2 led

```
  N
W   E
  S
```

♠ K Q J 4
♡ 10 5
♢ K J 6
♣ A J 9 2

The bidding goes:

South	West	North	East
1♣	No	1♡	No
1NT	No	3♡	No
3NT	No	No	No

'West leads the 2 of diamonds. East wins with the ace and returns the 4. How do you play?'

I temporized with a comment about South's rebid of 1NT in preference to one spade. Was three hearts forcing? Were the opponents strong players? Apparently they were.

'In that case,' I said, 'the danger of ducking the diamond is that West might win and switch to clubs. Then, if the heart finesse was wrong, I would lose at least five tricks. So I win the second diamond and run the 10 of hearts.'

Zia filled in the full diagram with unconcealed pleasure.

♠ A 2
♡ A K J 9 8 4
♢ 9 5 3
♣ 6 4

♠ 9 8 7 5
♡ 7 6
♢ 8 2
♣ Q 10 7 5 3

♠ 10 6 3
♡ Q 3 2
♢ A Q 10 7 4
♣ K 8

♠ K Q J 4
♡ 10 5
♢ K J 6
♣ A J 9 2

'I don't think you need blame yourself,' I said consolingly. 'West's lead of the 2 of diamonds was a brilliant deceptive stroke.'

Zia smiled. 'Thank you,' he said. 'I was West.'

Mr Grosvenor's whimsical diversions

The Grosvenor coup seems to have been around for quite a while, but it is a comparatively new addition to the bridge vocabulary. It was first described in the early nineteen-seventies.

The term describes situations where a defender may play a card that seems foolish but can hardly cost. For example:

```
              J 7 6 4
    2                      Q 10 9
              A K 8 5 3
```

Having some reason to place East rather than West with length in the suit, South leads the jack from dummy. If the distribution is 3–1 he has a better chance to pin a singleton 10 or 9 than to drop a singleton queen in the West hand. East can be sure of a trick, of course, but suppose he contributes a whimsical 10: South will read him for 10 9 possibly, but not for Q 10 9. Similarly:

```
              A 10 7 5 2
    Q J 4                   8
              K 9 6 3
```

If West drops the queen under the king and follows with the 4 on the next round, South will hardly finesse the 10.

Clever players have been known to play a Grosvenor deliberately – to make the declarer feel a little foolish. 'Dicing with death,' Zia calls it.

There are many situations where the distinction between a Grosvenor and a genuine deceptive play is narrow.

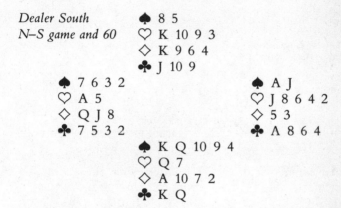

Q 10 4 2

9 8 6 3   K J

A 7 5

If East plays the jack under the ace, declarer may duck the next round and so make three tricks. East may try the king on the first round, a semi–Grosvenor. This may induce the declarer to insert dummy's 10 on the second round.

Sometimes a Grosvenor leads to a result that is difficult to foresee.

Dealer South ♠ 8 5
N–S game and 60 ♡ K 10 9 3
  ◇ K 9 6 4
  ♣ J 10 9

♠ 7 6 3 2   ♠ A J
♡ A 5   ♡ J 8 6 4 2
◇ Q J 8   ◇ 5 3
♣ 7 5 3 2   ♣ A 8 6 4

  ♠ K Q 10 9 4
  ♡ Q 7
  ◇ A 10 7 2
  ♣ K Q

South played in three diamonds, a game bid, and West began with ace and another heart. South, by no means a skilful performer, led the ace of diamonds at trick three, and West, seeing little prospect of defeating the contract by ordinary means, dropped the queen. Fearing J x x x of trumps on his right, South did not play another round, but switched to the queen of clubs. East won and led a low heart.

'Oh well,' the declarer thought to himself, 'West has dropped the queen of diamonds from Q x. I had better try the 10 of diamonds, because I can't afford to lose two trump tricks.'

The 10 of diamonds was overruffed by the jack. East came in with the ace of spades and led another heart. This time, West overruffed the 7 of diamonds with the 8; it was a sad affair.

The worst that can happen to a Grosvenor man is to find an opponent who simply refuses to draw the obvious conclusions.

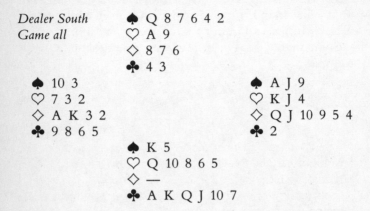

Dealer South
Game all

♠ Q 8 7 6 4 2
♡ A 9
♢ 8 7 6
♣ 4 3

♠ 10 3
♡ 7 3 2
♢ A K 3 2
♣ 9 8 6 5

♠ A J 9
♡ K J 4
♢ Q J 10 9 5 4
♣ 2

♠ K 5
♡ Q 10 8 6 5
♢ —
♣ A K Q J 10 7

South was a player who called a spade a spade in the broad accents of the West Riding. After an auction too horrible to describe, he arrived in four hearts. Having ruffed the diamond lead, he crossed blithely to the ace of hearts. East, recognizing that the only hope was to evoke some imaginary spectre, dropped the *king*.

This ruse might have caused a good player to waver, but South treated it with the disdain of a tank running over a bramble bush. 'Nothing to do if the hearts are 5–1,' he remarked. He led a second heart from dummy, and when East followed suit he reflected for a while, perhaps calculating that if West held J x x x in trumps it would not help him to play the queen. (West would have the tempo and South would not be able to make a spade trick.) In the end he finessed the 10 of hearts, drew the queen, and made six.

'Don't worry about missing slam, lad,' he consoled his partner. 'T'was better to take brass.'

7

Soldierly tactics, but no live ammunition

Sheehan, Rose, Coyle, and Shenkin, four members of the team that later represented Britain in the 1984 Olympiad at Seattle, played a practice match against the nucleus of the Italian team. The British quartet was reinforced by Dixon and Silverstone, who were unlucky not to have been selected.

It would be an exaggeration to describe the match as light-hearted, but it was a little like a military exercise without live ammunition. The home side led after the first two sessions, but failed to resist a strong Italian charge in the final session.

If British supporters were mildly disappointed by the narrow defeat, there was unexpected reassurance in the British superiority at slam level. This is a department of the game where British teams have habitually lost points to the Italians. Sheehan and Rose gained no fewer than four slam swings. This was one of them:

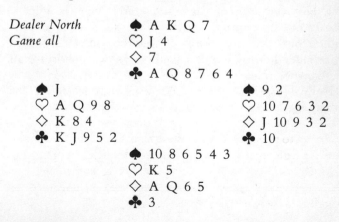

Dealer North   ♠ A K Q 7
Game all   ♡ J 4
              ◇ 7
              ♣ A Q 8 7 6 4

♠ J   ♠ 9 2
♡ A Q 9 8   ♡ 10 7 6 3 2
◇ K 8 4   ◇ J 10 9 3 2
♣ K J 9 5 2   ♣ 10

              ♠ 10 8 6 5 4 3
              ♡ K 5
              ◇ A Q 6 5
              ♣ 3

South	West	North	East
Rose	De Falco	Sheehan	Garozzo
—	—	1♣	No
1♠	No	2♡[1]	No
3♢	No	4♠	No
5♠[2]	No	6♠[3]	No
No	No		

[1] A direct raise to four spades would be uninformative. An advantage of two hearts – if you play the reverse as forcing – is that the subsequent raise in spades will convey the diamond shortage.

[2] In this type of sequence five spades conveys the question: Are your trumps really good?

[3] 24-carat is the answer.

West led the jack of spades to dummy's ace. Declarer set about establishing the clubs, beginning with ace and another, as the slam would be guaranteed if the clubs were not worse than 4–2. Now Garozzo (for once) made a slight error: he ruffed the second club with the 9 of spades.

Rose overruffed, cashed the ace of diamonds and ruffed a diamond. A club ruff and another diamond ruff dislodged the king of diamonds. Now he was able to discard one of dummy's hearts on the queen of diamonds and establish dummy's clubs. If Garozzo had preserved his 9 of spades dummy would have been an entry short for all these manoeuvres.

Benito may lack the Sicilian's traditional thirst for revenge, but he invariably gets his own back.

Dealer South
Game all

	♠ Q 6	
	♡ A 10 8 3	
	◇ 8 7 6	
	♣ K 7 6 4	

♠ 10 9		♠ K J 5 4
♡ 4		♡ J 9 6 5
◇ A Q J 10 3 2		◇ 5 4
♣ 10 9 8 2		♣ Q J 3

	♠ A 8 7 3 2	
	♡ K Q 7 2	
	◇ K 9	
	♣ A 5	

South	West	North	East
Garozzo	Rose	De Falco	Sheehan
1NT[1]	No	2♣	No
2♡	No	3♡	No
4♡	dble[2]	No	No
No			

[1] Benito's story is that the 2 of spades somehow nestled among his clubs.

[2] A typical Rose gambit. The opponents' bidding shows that they are limited. Rose knows that the trumps will break badly and hopes that declarer will encounter other distributional storms.

South won the club lead and played a spade to the 10, queen and king. East returned the ◇ 5. It appears automatic to play the king, but Garozzo inserted the 9. However, Rose had too many diamonds to be deceived; he continued with ace and another, South ruffing.

Realizing that there was not room for West to hold long hearts, the declarer played king of hearts and a heart to the ace, followed by a low spade from the table. At this point black comedy intervened. Sheehan played the jack of spades (unnecessary but not fatal), but when Garozzo won with the ace and returned the 8, ruffing low in dummy, the defender 'overruffed' with the 9 of hearts. This became a penalty card, so that when the fifth spade was ruffed with ♡10 Rob had to underruff and the contract was made.

Part of Benito's magic, you see, lies in inducing the most consistent and level-headed opponent to misplay.

8

A rose by any other name

Even bridge players would concede that chess enjoys the richer language. Our squeezes, end-plays, and throw-ins, seem flat and clinical when compared with the euphony of the Ruy Lopez, the Sicilian and the Fianchetto. As for the names of our systems, CAB, Precision, Acol, Utility – these have the melody of a pneumatic drill and the poetry of an income-tax form.

To be fair, there are some plays with names which do at least present a good visual picture – for example, the Crocodile Coup and the Stepping-Stone Squeeze (both named by Terence Reese, I believe). The following deal is an example of a crocodile that failed to open its jaws.

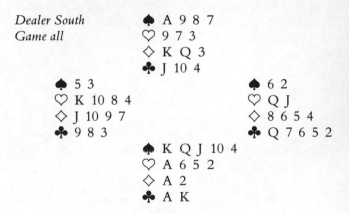

Dealer South
Game all

♠ A 9 8 7
♡ 9 7 3
♢ K Q 3
♣ J 10 4

♠ 5 3
♡ K 10 8 4
♢ J 10 9 7
♣ 9 8 3

♠ 6 2
♡ Q J
♢ 8 6 5 4
♣ Q 7 6 5 2

♠ K Q J 10 4
♡ A 6 5 2
♢ A 2
♣ A K

South	West	North	East
2♠[1]	No	3♠	No
4♣	No	4♦	No
4♥	No	5♠[2]	No
6♠	No	No	No

[1] This is a rather awkward type in the Acol system. I would prefer two clubs, with 2NT as an inferior alternative.

[2] He has extra values – good trumps and the honours in the minor suits.

West led the jack of diamonds and first sight of the dummy was not reassuring. It seemed that the queen of diamonds and the jack of clubs would not pull their weight.

The only genuine chance was to find a defender with a holding in hearts such as king single or doubleton K Q. To make it more difficult for a defender with a doubleton king of hearts to unblock, it is good play to lead to the ace of hearts early on. Thus a fair sequence is to draw two trumps, play a heart to the ace, and then eliminate the minor suits. This leads to:

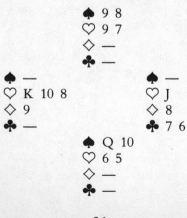

South led a heart and West, who had noted his partner's queen on the first round of the suit, played the 10. This was a small tragedy, because his partner was left on play, forced to concede a ruff-and-discard.

'Have you ever met a baby crocodile?' East asked the world.

'It wasn't so easy,' West replied. 'If you had held Q x of hearts it would have been right to play the queen on the first round.'

Yes, I suppose that's true. West placed his partner with Q x and South with A J x x, though with this holding South would probably have played the first heart from dummy.

You might call the next hand either a stepping-stone or a squeeze-without-the-count.

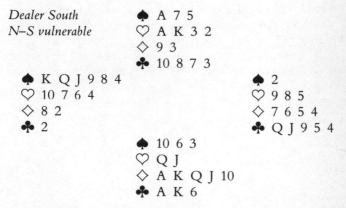

Dealer South
N–S vulnerable

♠ A 7 5
♡ A K 3 2
♢ 9 3
♣ 10 8 7 3

♠ K Q J 9 8 4
♡ 10 7 6 4
♢ 8 2
♣ 2

♠ 2
♡ 9 8 5
♢ 7 6 5 4
♣ Q J 9 5 4

♠ 10 6 3
♡ Q J
♢ A K Q J 10
♣ A K 6

Some twenty years ago I played a series of tournaments in America, partnered by Peter Pender, who is now one of their top internationals, winning the World Championship at São Paulo in 1985. Peter was South on this deal and he played in six diamonds after West had made a weak jump overcall of two spades.

West led the king of spades and South had to win. After four rounds of diamonds and two of clubs the position was:

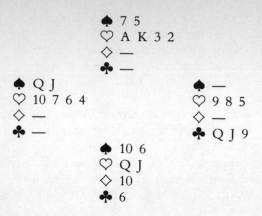

♠ 7 5
♡ A K 3 2
♢ —
♣ —

♠ Q J   ♠ —
♡ 10 7 6 4   ♡ 9 8 5
♢ —   ♢ —
♣ —   ♣ Q J 9

♠ 10 6
♡ Q J
♢ 10
♣ 6

The last diamond forced West to throw a spade. A spade is thrown from dummy and South can make the contract in two ways: lead a spade (a squeeze-without-the-count), or cash Q J of hearts and follow with a spade (a stepping-stone).

9

When midgets don the lion's skin

Since I first started a small campaign against pointless jump bids by the weaker side, I have come across many deals that support my ideas on this subject. This one is from an American international trial.

Dealer North ♠ A Q J 6 4 2
N–S vulnerable ♡ K
◇ Q 10 7 2
♣ A 4

♠ 5   ♠ 10 9 8 7
♡ J 10 8 7   ♡ Q 6 5 4
◇ 3   ◇ A J 8
♣ Q J 10 8 7 6 2   ♣ K 5

♠ K 3
♡ A 9 3 2
◇ K 9 6 5 4
♣ 9 3

South	West	North	East
—	—	1♠	No
2◇	4♣[1]	5♣	No
5♡[2]	No	6◇	No
No	No		

[1] This feeble cry can hardly gain.
[2] Accepting partner's slam suggestion.

West led the queen of clubs and dummy won. To obtain a discard on the ace of hearts, South had to cash the king, enter hand with the king of spades, and discard dummy's losing club. Then he played a diamond to the queen and ace.

Some players in East's position would have returned a spade at this point, exposing partner's lack of a second trump. East was not so foolish: he led a club, but South, remembering West's four-club bid, finessed in trumps and made the slam.

At the other table there was a small comedy of a different kind. The bidding went:

South	West	North	East
—	—	1♠	No
1NT[1]	3♣[2]	3♠	No
4♠	5♣	dble	No
No	No		

[1] This was forcing for one round.
[2] The jump was not quite so foolish as in the previous sequence.

North led the king of hearts and switched to a low diamond. Declarer won with the ace in dummy and followed with the 8 of diamonds at trick two. Knowing that his partner held the queen, South played low. This was a mistake, because West took the opportunity to dispose of his spade loser. Now North could not give his partner the lead and West escaped for two down instead of three down.

A couple of years ago I played in a British team at the Epson tournament in Japan. The main event was for international teams of four. The following hand passed off quietly enough at my table:

```
              ♠ A 9 5
              ♡ 7
              ◇ K J 10 7 2
              ♣ 7 5 4 3
♠ J 6 4 2                        ♠ K Q 7
♡ K Q 9 6 2                      ♡ 5
◇ 9 8                            ◇ A Q 5 4
♣ K J                            ♣ A Q 10 6 2
              ♠ 10 8 3
              ♡ A J 10 8 4 3
              ◇ 6 3
              ♣ 9 8
```

At game all West became declarer in 3NT and made
eleven tricks. There was no swing in our match. I was
surprised to read later that six South players had lost
upwards of 1100 in two hearts doubled. Nick Hughes, a
member of the Australian team, described the bidding at
his own table:

South	West	North	East
—	—	No	No
2♡	No	No	dble
No	No	No	

The Australian East–West pair were playing strong
passes, and South fell into the mire. Hughes wrote: 'This
catastrophe cost Panama a place in the final, but I
sympathize with South; the long-term cost of failing to bid
such hands over big clubs or forcing passes is surely
greater.'

What rubbish! Your side is never going to obtain the
contract for a reasonable score, and meanwhile you make
the play much easier for the opposition if you end up
defending.

Weak jump overcalls have one advantage: they deprive

opponents of one round of bidding. The advantage is reduced by the modern use of negative doubles. They have three disadvantages: they give opponents a picture of the layout; they deprive the defending side of a descriptive bid on strong one-suited hands; and occasionally, as on this last deal, they concede a big penalty.

10

Stifled under the security blanket

Tournament bridge today is barely recognizable as the largely informal but invariably decorous game we played twenty or thirty years ago. Some of the innovations are restricted to bridge at the summit, others have become established as part of the duplicate game at all levels.

Players have become accustomed to the regulation that they should say 'Stop' or 'Skip bid' when they propose to make a jump bid of any kind. Few know the origin of this ruling. During the European Championship at Montreux in 1954 the scorers were asked to call 'Stop' when there was a pre-emptive jump, such as three hearts over an opening one club. There was some sense in this. However, many of the scorers were not bridge players at all and were unable to distinguish between one type of jump and another. So the instruction was given: Call 'Stop' whenever there is a jump of any kind. This, before long, became a general ruling, so that nowadays we have the ridiculous practice of a player calling 'Stop' when he advances from 4NT to 6NT.

Worse still, bridge at international level is conducted behind screens. During the bidding a contraption across the table separates North and East from South and West, the idea being twofold: that partners should not be able to exchange any signals, and that players should not derive information from undue hesitations. The system requires monitors, who silently pass a chit to the next two players, showing the calls that have been made. Needless to say, one practically always knows, from the logic of the bidding, who has taken time – partner or opponent.

The first appearance of these screens at world championship level was not without black humour. The occasion was the world championship of 1975. The Americans, always suspicious of their rivals at the top, felt the screens would enable them to establish their superiority.

The atmosphere was frosty from the first and became icy when two of the less-renowned Italian players were accused of exchanging signals with their *feet*. After the usual brouhaha the World Bridge Federation delivered its customary inconclusive verdict. Unable to find any correlation between the kicks under the table and the bidding and play, they reprimanded the Italian pair and found them guilty of 'improper foot movements'. Blocks were placed under the table to prevent any further communication. The Americans, who lost to the Italians once again, found the verdict a trifle unsatisfactory.

The truth is that most expert players are honest in their intentions and skilful in not giving unfair information to their partners. Also, the partners are well trained in not acting on information they may have gained in an improper way. Any pair that fails to maintain these standards is quickly identified. Average players, on the other hand, commonly convey, and act upon, information that is not part of the game. One just has to put up with it.

Before I leave this subject, let me say that bidding boxes, which enable players to indicate all their bids without speaking, have no disadvantages at all in an ethical sense. Also, they make it much easier for spectators to follow the game.

Sometimes it is difficult to maintain a straight face when partner puts down a completely unsuitable, or at any rate unexpected, dummy. John Wignall managed it on this deal when New Zealand played Mexico in the Olympiad:

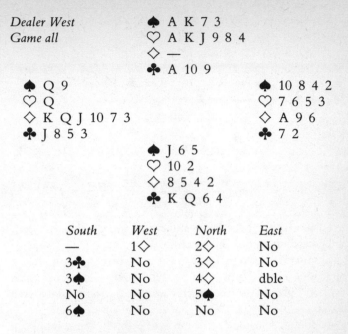

Dealer West
Game all

North:
♠ A K 7 3
♡ A K J 9 8 4
♢ —
♣ A 10 9

West:
♠ Q 9
♡ Q
♢ K Q J 10 7 3
♣ J 8 5 3

East:
♠ 10 8 4 2
♡ 7 6 5 3
♢ A 9 6
♣ 7 2

South:
♠ J 6 5
♡ 10 2
♢ 8 5 4 2
♣ K Q 6 4

South	West	North	East
—	1◇	2♡	No
3♣	No	3◇	No
3♠	No	4◇	dble
No	No	5♠	No
6♣	No	No	No

I think that if I had been South I would have thrown a
brick at a partner who after this auction put down just four
trumps, due to become three when the diamond lead was
ruffed.

The situation improved slightly when the ace and king
of spades brought down the queen and the queen of hearts
appeared on the first round. If the declarer plays off the
hearts now, East will not ruff but will dispose of his club
losers. Wignall made the critical play of cashing king and
queen of clubs. Then, after three more rounds of hearts the
position was:

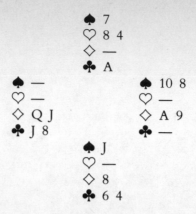

```
            ♠ 7
            ♡ 8 4
            ◇ —
            ♣ A
♠ —                      ♠ 10 8
♡ —                      ♡ —
◇ Q J                    ◇ A 9
♣ J 8                    ♣ —
            ♠ J
            ♡ —
            ◇ 8
            ♣ 6 4
```

East ruffs the next heart and South may either overruff or discard; the result is the same.

If you thought this play was not too difficult, don't mention it next time you are in Mexico. The Mexican declarer played in the same contract and finished two down.

11

Failure leads to ruffled feathers

Playing a cross-ruff provides the same sort of carefree exhilaration as riding a bicycle for the first time. It is only with experience that you learn it is dangerous to relax your grip on the handlebars.

Dealer East
N–S vulnerable

	♠ K Q 10 7	
	♡ 3	
	◇ Q 8 4	
	♣ A K 7 5 4	

♠ 4 3		♠ J 2
♡ K Q 10 8 6		♡ 9 2
◇ J 10 9		◇ K 7 5 3
♣ J 9 2		♣ Q 10 8 6 3

	♠ A 9 8 6 5	
	♡ A J 7 5 4	
	◇ A 6 2	
	♣ —	

South	West	North	East
—	—	—	No
1♠	No	3♣[1]	No
3♡	No	3♠	No
4◇	No	4♠[2]	No
6♠	No	No	No

[1] The North hand is just too strong for a delayed game raise – two clubs, followed by four spades.

[2] I must say that I would have hazarded either four hearts or five spades at this point, but evidently North set a high standard for his original force.

West led the jack of diamonds and South tried the queen from dummy. When this was covered by the king and ace, he cashed ace of hearts, ruffed a heart, and discarded two diamonds on the ace and king of clubs. After a diamond ruff the position was:

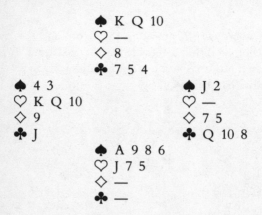

At this point South led a low heart and West played a slightly deceptive king. South tried the 10 of spades from dummy; East overruffed with the jack and meanly returned a trump, leaving South a trick short.

In the diagram position South needs only one low ruff to be sure of twelve tricks. He should have ruffed the third heart with the queen of spades, then a club with the 9 of spades. When this survives, as after all is likely, he can ruff a heart with the king of spades and a club with the ace. Now he loses only to the jack of spades.

The next hand was a little more difficult, because the declarer had to change direction half-way through the play.

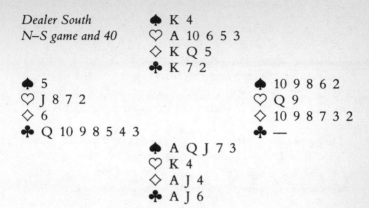

Dealer South
N–S game and 40

♠ K 4
♡ A 10 6 5 3
◇ K Q 5
♣ K 7 2

♠ 5   ♠ 10 9 8 6 2
♡ J 8 7 2   ♡ Q 9
◇ 6   ◇ 10 9 8 7 3 2
♣ Q 10 9 8 5 4 3   ♣ —

♠ A Q J 7 3
♡ K 4
◇ A J 4
♣ A J 6

The opening bid on the South hand is a trifle awkward at 40 up. One spade, two spades, 2NT? South chose two spades, as this is not unconditionally forcing when enough for game. The bidding continued:

South	West	North	East
2♠	No	3♡	No
3NT	No	6♠	No
No	No		

North's six spades was a trifle hasty, but from a part score one tends not to investigate grand slams. 6NT might have been better.

South won the diamond lead with the jack, mentally chalking up a sizeable rubber. He then played a spade to the king and a spade back. Prospects were not good when West discarded a club.

Floundering a little, South played king and ace of hearts. If the hearts are 3–3 the play is easy, but when a normally guileless East dropped the queen of hearts on the second round, the prospect of a 3–3 break receded. Changing his plan, South aimed to make his 7 of spades *en passant*; that is to say, he planned to cash the minor-suit winners and be in dummy to lead a heart at trick twelve, so establishing a trick for his last trump.

Pursuing this plan, South crossed to hand with a diamond, on which West discarded another club. Then a club to the king was ruffed, East exited with a third diamond, and South had no way to dispose of his club loser.

This was a poor effort by a supposed good player. When West showed out on the second diamond, the way was clear: aim for a squeeze against West in hearts and clubs. After two more rounds of trumps the position is:

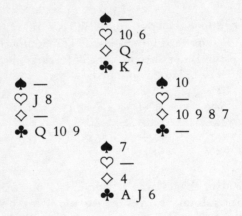

South leads his last trump and West parts with a heart. Now a diamond lead from East is more than West can bear.

12

Different play of twin holdings

'Slams may hit the headlines, but matches are won and lost in the part-score battles.' I remember reading a pronouncement of that kind when I was a novice in the tournament world. This is not so much the case today, because of the general improvement in bidding. But it is still possible to win matches by accurate play on the small hands. Two examples follow where, by a curious chance, a team lost points on two occasions through the mishandling of an identical holding in clubs.

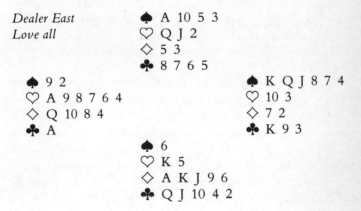

Dealer East
Love all

♠ A 10 5 3
♡ Q J 2
♢ 5 3
♣ 8 7 6 5

♠ 9 2
♡ A 9 8 7 6 4
♢ Q 10 8 4
♣ A

♠ K Q J 8 7 4
♡ 10 3
♢ 7 2
♣ K 9 3

♠ 6
♡ K 5
♢ A K J 9 6
♣ Q J 10 4 2

South	West	North	East
—	—	—	2♦[1]
3♦	dble[2]	No	No
4♣[3]	No	No	No

[1] The multicoloured two-diamond opening, usually representing a weak two in one of the majors.

[2] As a rule, I approve of doubling the bid you know you can defeat, but the position is a little different when partner has opened with a semi-pre-empt; on such occasions the opponents often benefit from a second chance.

[3] And this is what happens here.

West began with the ace and another heart. South, who had unblocked the king on the first round, won in dummy and played a club to the queen and ace. West led a third heart; East ruffed with the 9 and South overruffed. There were still three trumps in dummy, so the declarer had no difficulty in ruffing two diamonds and making his contract.

'Did you have to ruff the third heart?' West demanded. 'I gave you a chance to discard a diamond.'

As East held the 9 of clubs and could overruff the dummy, it wasn't even necessary for him to discard a diamond on the third heart. Note, however, that if East's clubs had been the K 4 3 the discard of a diamond on the third heart would have been a necessary, and a winning, play. It is an unusual hand, a sort of loser-on-loser by the defence.

This type of play is not unknown, however, and I think that the mistake made later in the match by West was more forgivable.

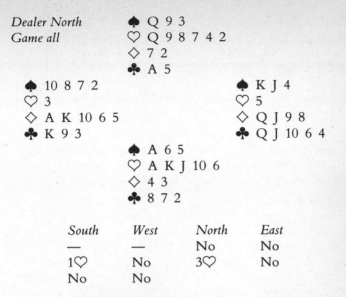

Dealer North
Game all

	♠ Q 9 3	
	♡ Q 9 8 7 4 2	
	◇ 7 2	
	♣ A 5	

♠ 10 8 7 2		♠ K J 4
♡ 3		♡ 5
◇ A K 10 6 5		◇ Q J 9 8
♣ K 9 3		♣ Q J 10 6 4

	♠ A 6 5	
	♡ A K J 10 6	
	◇ 4 3	
	♣ 8 7 2	

South	West	North	East
—	—	No	No
1♡	No	3♡	No
No	No		

It was a good pass of three hearts. Many players would say, 'I had three quick tricks and good trumps.' Here the good trumps became less of an asset in view of North's raise to three, and these 5–3–3–2 hands are not powerful in the play.

West began with a high diamond, East played the queen, and West continued with a low diamond to his partner's jack. East switched to the queen of clubs and dummy's ace won the second round. South came to hand with a trump, ruffed his third club, and led another trump. Then he led a low spade and inserted dummy's 9. East won but was now on play, forced to return a spade or concede a ruff-and-discard.

Perhaps West should have tried a spade at trick two, as he could see that two spade tricks would be needed to beat the contract. However that may be, he had a better chance later. It was essential to overtake partner's queen of clubs with the king; if this is allowed to hold, he switches to the 8 of spades.

Was East blameless? Not altogether. Suppose West's clubs had been K 8 3 instead of K 9 3; in that case a *low* club from East would be more effective than the queen, as it would ensure an entry for his partner.

13

Dunce's cap in commentators' corner

One of the lesser-known professions, in America at any rate, is that of bridge-writer-bashing. A correspondent in the *Bridge World* drew attention to a number of inaccurate comments by celebrated columnists (or their ghost writers). The horrible thing was that the critic seemed to be right in all cases. Here are two of them:

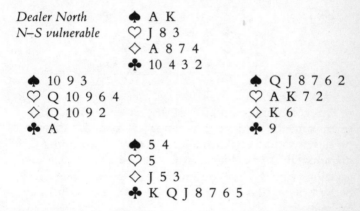

Dealer North
N–S vulnerable

♠ A K
♡ J 8 3
♢ A 8 7 4
♣ 10 4 3 2

♠ 10 9 3
♡ Q 10 9 6 4
♢ Q 10 9 2
♣ A

♠ Q J 8 7 6 2
♡ A K 7 2
♢ K 6
♣ 9

♠ 5 4
♡ 5
♢ J 5 3
♣ K Q J 8 7 6 5

North–South defended in five clubs against four hearts, expecting to go only one down. 'This,' observed the columnist, 'they would have achieved but for East's careful discarding.' What happened was that after two rounds of hearts, a club to the ace and another heart, South played a diamond to the ace. East cleverly unblocked the king, so that when South cashed the spades and exited with a diamond, the defence took two diamond tricks and scored 500.

Anything wrong with that? Only that if South delays the play of the trump suit until he has eliminated the other suits, East's unblock of the diamond king does not help the defence. As soon as this card appears, the declarer plays a club to West's ace and is only one down.

Another example:

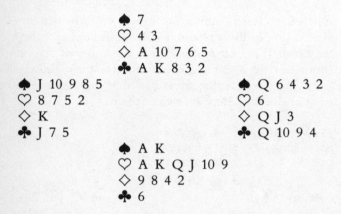

```
              ♠ 7
              ♡ 4 3
              ◇ A 10 7 6 5
              ♣ A K 8 3 2
♠ J 10 9 8 5              ♠ Q 6 4 3 2
♡ 8 7 5 2                ♡ 6
◇ K                      ◇ Q J 3
♣ J 7 5                  ♣ Q 10 9 4
              ♠ A K
              ♡ A K Q J 10 9
              ◇ 9 8 4 2
              ♣ 6
```

The columnist pointed out that in six hearts, after a spade lead, the declarer should not rely on a 2–2 diamond break but should establish a long club, thus obtaining two diamond discards. He added, 'The king of diamonds opening would have doomed the contract inevitably, because it would have removed a vital entry from the table.'

Not 'inevitably'. South may duck on the opening lead, and then again he has enough entries to dummy to establish a long club.

Mind you, the critics are sometimes a little harsh. I remember once writing about this deal from a match between India and Australia. It became known as the Great Indian Cross-ruff.

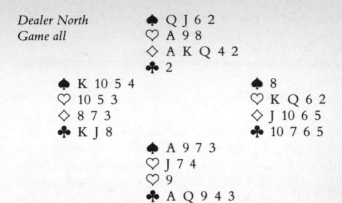

Dealer North
Game all

♠ Q J 6 2
♡ A 9 8
♢ A K Q 4 2
♣ 2

♠ K 10 5 4   ♠ 8
♡ 10 5 3   ♡ K Q 6 2
♢ 8 7 3   ♢ J 10 6 5
♣ K J 8   ♣ 10 7 6 5

♠ A 9 7 3
♡ J 7 4
♡ 9
♣ A Q 9 4 3

The Australian North, playing in five spades, took finesses here and there and somehow managed to go three down. The Indian South played in six spades against a diamond lead. He discarded two hearts on the top diamonds and did a spot of cross-ruffing, to reach this ending:

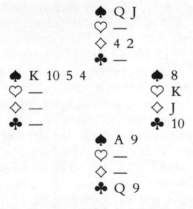

♠ Q J
♡ —
♢ 4 2
♣ —

♠ K 10 5 4   ♠ 8
♡ —   ♡ K
♢ —   ♢ J
♣ —   ♣ 10

♠ A 9
♡ —
♢ —
♣ Q 9

South leads the queen of clubs and West makes only one trick. Even a trump lead doesn't beat it, I incautiously observed. About three months later I had a letter from India: 'West must be leading king of spades,' it said. 'Then South is not making slam.'

14

Such stuff as nightmares are made on

In 1937 Ely Culbertson, accompanied by his wife, Josephine, Helen Sobel and Charles C. Vogelhofer, set forth for Budapest to defend the world championship (so called) which the United States had won in New York in 1935. Culbertson had won championship matches both in America and Britain – against, it was said, opponents whom he had selected himself.

To Culbertson's chagrin, he lost to the European champions, Austria, by the considerable margin of 4,740 points. However deflated the Americans may have been, the result was no fluke. The Austrian team, which contained the legendary pair of Schneider and Jellinek and was captained by Paul Stern, were all magnificent card players.

Some of these great players survived, but not all. Jellinek 'disappeared' in Norway. Herbert escaped to America and had a distinguished career in music. Stern came to England, accompanied by the romantic story that he was eleventh on the Nazi hit list and had returned his Iron Cross, from the First World War, to the German High Command. Von Bludhorn lived in Paris from 1938 to 1960. Schneider, though in poor health, continued to play in Austrian teams during the 1950s.

When Schneider and his post-war partner, Reithoffer, ceased to be available, Austria became an irregular competitor in European and world championships. In the 1980s they began to show signs of their old form. No one thought of Austria as a likely winner of the Olympiad at Seattle, but after seventeen rounds they led their Group and qualified in third place. Their opponents in the quarter-final were the mighty Americans. Austria won a closely contested match and in the semifinal was drawn against Poland, another team that has come to the fore in recent years.

Austria was ahead for most of the match, but the difference was only 3 IMPs when the last board was shown on the screen:

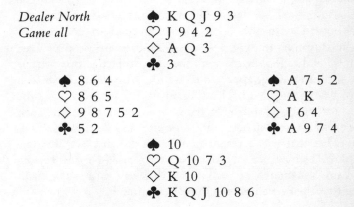

Dealer North
Game all

♠ K Q J 9 3
♡ J 9 4 2
♢ A Q 3
♣ 3

♠ 8 6 4   ♠ A 7 5 2
♡ 8 6 5   ♡ A K
♢ 9 8 7 5 2   ♢ J 6 4
♣ 5 2   ♣ A 9 7 4

♠ 10
♡ Q 10 7 3
♢ K 10
♣ K Q J 10 8 6

In the closed room the Polish North–South played in four hearts doubled and lost the obvious four tricks; 200 to Austria, and it seemed to be all over.

This was the bidding on bridgerama:

South	West	North	East
—	—	2◇	dble
2NT	No	3◇	No
4♡	No	No	dble
No	No	No	

It looks as though North's two-diamond opening signified a major two-suiter, and perhaps the bid of three diamonds on the second round indicated the 'fragment'. I could be wrong. East's double is easier to understand.

49

West led the ♣ 5 to his partner's ace. East cashed the ace of spades and, like a jockey who has safely negotiated the final hurdle, continued with a second spade.

Now international bridge players seldom suffer from nerves. The cry of those ghastly TV commentators, 'the pressure is getting to him', has no meaning in bridge. Or so I would have thought. But the declarer, Milares (too late to spare names), made the weird play of ruffing the second spade in hand. He made another slip when he followed with the 10 of hearts instead of crossing to dummy and leading a low trump from the table. East headed the 10 of hearts with the king and led a third spade.

Still in a daze, apparently, South ruffed with the queen of hearts, then led his last heart to the 9 and ace. Now the fourth spade established a trick for West's 8 of hearts. Two down, 500 to Poland, 7 match points, and Austria had lost.

The final was a runaway win for Poland over France. Journalists wrote of an exhausted, out-of-form French team; the match records tell a different story; the truth is that the French played in really bad luck.

15

Times when peasants outplay princes

It has been suggested that the reason why Russian officialdom disapproves of bridge lies in the royalist imagery of the playing-cards themselves.

Perhaps the two hands that follow would reassure them that the lowly peasants sometimes have a role to play.

```
Dealer South          ♠ K 8 6
E–W vulnerable        ♡ 9 6 3
                      ◇ A J 3
                      ♣ 7 6 5 2
  ♠ 7 5                            ♠ J 10 9 3 2
  ♡ K Q J 7 2                      ♡ 8 4
  ◇ 10 9 8                         ◇ Q 7 6 5 4
  ♣ J 4 3                          ♣ K
                      ♠ A Q 4
                      ♡ A 10 5
                      ◇ K 2
                      ♣ A Q 10 9 8
```

South	West	North	East
1♣[1]	No	1◇[2]	No
3NT	No	No	No

[1] You would have opened 2NT? So would I.
[2] As good as anything; it might be a mistake to respond 1NT with such bald holdings in the major suits.

West led the king of hearts and followed with the queen. When South played low again, West continued with the

2 of hearts. East discarded the 4 of diamonds and South won.

The declarer's next move was the ace of clubs. He was unable then to establish the suit without letting West into the lead; one down, and his partner was disappointed.

Three mistakes were made during the early play of this hand. Could you name them all?

First, it was silly of South to hold up the ace of hearts for a third round. If the opposing hearts are 5–2 nothing is gained by holding up and it may be helpful to retain a card of exit. If the hearts are 4–3, then South can afford to lose a club and three hearts.

Second, if East had ever read a book he would have known (a) that his partner's 2 of hearts indicated a possible entry in clubs, and (b) that singleton aces, kings and queens are often dangerous cards to keep. He should have thrown the king of clubs on the third heart.

Third, after his mistake in holding up twice in hearts South could have recovered by entering dummy for the first lead of clubs. When East plays the king he is allowed to hold the trick.

The 2 of hearts was a significant card on the last hand. This time it's the 2 of diamonds.

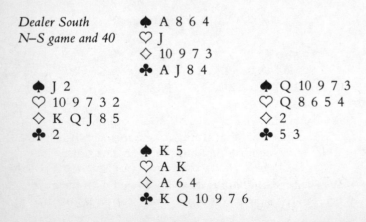

Dealer South
N–S game and 40

♠ A 8 6 4
♡ J
♢ 10 9 7 3
♣ A J 8 4

♠ J 2
♡ 10 9 7 3 2
♢ K Q J 8 5
♣ 2

♠ Q 10 9 7 3
♡ Q 8 6 5 4
♢ 2
♣ 5 3

♠ K 5
♡ A K
♢ A 6 4
♣ K Q 10 9 7 6

South	West	North	East
1♣[1]	1◇	1♠[2]	No
3♣[3]	No	4♣	No
6♣	No	No	No

[1] You would have opened 2NT? So would I.
[2] You would have raised to three clubs? So would I.
[3] He has 40 below, remember, so this is reasonable.

West led the king of diamonds, East played the 2, and South won. He drew trumps, then played what in some circles is called a 'golf club squeeze'; that is to say, he played off all his winners, hoping that something would develop. On this occasion it was scarcely possible for the defence to go wrong.

You see why the 2 of diamonds was important? So long as West has five diamonds and East only one, and so long as East holds at least four spades, the contract is cast-iron. South should play for this ending:

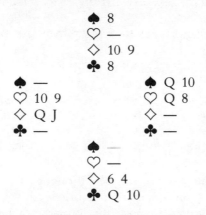

```
                    ♠ 8
                    ♡ —
                    ◇ 10 9
                    ♣ 8
    ♠ —                         ♠ Q 10
    ♡ 10 9                      ♡ Q 8
    ◇ Q J                       ◇ —
    ♣ —                         ♣ —
                    ♠ —
                    ♡ —
                    ◇ 6 4
                    ♣ Q 10
```

The lead is in dummy and the 8 of spades, on which South discards a diamond, leaves East on play.

16

Double, double, toil and trouble

'I doubled on the bidding.' So they often say, and I do it myself at rubber bridge. Sometimes it's not so clever.

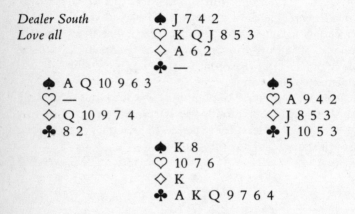

Dealer South
Love all

♠ J 7 4 2
♡ K Q J 8 5 3
◇ A 6 2
♣ —

♠ A Q 10 9 6 3
♡ —
◇ Q 10 9 7 4
♣ 8 2

♠ 5
♡ A 9 4 2
◇ J 8 5 3
♣ J 10 5 3

♠ K 8
♡ 10 7 6
◇ K
♣ A K Q 9 7 6 4

I was East and the bidding went:

South	West	North	East
1♣	2♠	3♡	No
3NT[1]	No	No	dble[2]
redble	No	No	No[3]

[1] After some (very reasonable) thought.
[2] Foolishly concluding that South wasn't too happy. I
     thought it quite possible that North (not a great striker
     of the ball) would revert to four hearts.
[3] Feeling foolish, but what could I do?

West led the 10 of diamonds. South played two rounds of hearts, which I allowed to win, then ace and king of clubs. This left:

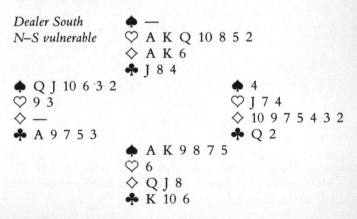

```
                    ♠ J 7 4
                    ♡ K Q 8 5
                    ◇ A
                    ♣ —
  ♠ A Q 10 9                      ♠ 5
  ♡ —                             ♡ A 9
  ◇ Q 9 7 4                       ◇ J 8 3
  ♣ —                             ♣ J 10
                    ♠ K 8
                    ♡ 10
                    ◇ —
                    ♣ Q 9 7 6 4
```

If South leads a heart in this tricky position we cannot beat him. Instead, he cashed the queen of clubs first and then played a heart to the queen and ace. Now I cashed the fourth club and *dummy* was squeezed. Try it!

The next deal, from an encounter between French and Spanish players in the Pairs Olympiad, produced a rather different result.

Dealer South
N–S vulnerable

```
                    ♠ —
                    ♡ A K Q 10 8 5 2
                    ◇ A K 6
                    ♣ J 8 4
  ♠ Q J 10 6 3 2                  ♠ 4
  ♡ 9 3                           ♡ J 7 4
  ◇ —                             ◇ 10 9 7 5 4 3 2
  ♣ A 9 7 5 3                     ♣ Q 2
                    ♠ A K 9 8 7 5
                    ♡ 6
                    ◇ Q J 8
                    ♣ K 10 6
```

55

When the French pair was North–South, the bidding went:

South	West	North	East
1♠	No	2♡	No
2♠	No	3♣	No
3NT	dble	redble	No
No	No		

West thought he had South's main suit sewn up. So he had, but North was there, too. West led a low club and South made thirteen tricks for the unusual score of 2550.

There was equal comedy and drama at another table where Chemla and Mari were East–West against another French pair.

South	West	North	East
1♠	No	3♡	4♢[1]
No	No	5♣[2]	No
5♡	No	6♡	No
No	dble	No	No
6♠	dble	6NT	No
No	dble	No	No
No			

[1] Preparing for a sacrifice against vulnerable opponents.
[2] I am told that this was an asking bid and that South's response (two steps) signified second-round control of clubs.

East led a spade to South's ace. Knowing that West was void of diamonds (remember East's four diamonds), North took a first-round finesse in hearts! East won and switched to a club.

Was that unlucky? Ye-es, but if North had thought of cashing a second spade he would have found that the spades were 6–1 and might have formed a different opinion about the hearts.

17

Discard of an honour conveys special message

If you lead an ace and partner follows with the king you will know – usually, at least – that he is pleased with you. But there is more than this to the language of discards. Study the defence on the two hands that follow.

Dealer South
Game all

	♠ A J 5	
	♡ 7 3	
	♢ K Q 10 6	
	♣ Q J 9 3	
♠ 9 8 7 3 2		♠ 6 4
♡ A 5		♡ Q J 10 9 6 2
♢ 7 5		♢ J 3 2
♣ K 10 8 2		♣ 6 5
	♠ K Q 10	
	♡ K 8 4	
	♢ A 9 8 4	
	♣ A 7 4	

South	West	North	East
1♣	No	1♢	No
1NT	No	3NT	No
No	No		

West led the 8 of spades (second best from a weak suit) and South won with the king. On four rounds of diamonds West discarded two spades, East the queen of hearts.

Declarer followed with the queen of clubs from dummy. West dropped the 8 – a fairly well-known type of false card. It achieved its object here when South followed with the jack from dummy, hoping to pin a doubleton 10 8. West won and returned a club to South's ace.

Calculating that the defence had given him nothing and that his little adventure in the club suit had cost a trick, South decided that he must recover by entering dummy with a spade and leading a heart towards the king. The defence took four heart tricks and South, who had started with nine tricks on top, was one down.

North pretended some astonishment as he inspected the travelling score-slip, which so far recorded six 660s, four 630s, one 600. 'Bad luck, partner.' North's sarcasm was justified, for while it is sometimes right in a pairs event to risk the contract unnecessarily, South on this occasion could have made sure of ten tricks by cashing the spades and exiting with a fourth round of clubs.

South's play was silly, but note the value of East's discard of the queen of hearts. This told partner that it would be safe to lead from the king but not from the ace.

But it's not always right to play the king from K Q, the queen from Q J. Sometimes you will need to convey a special message.

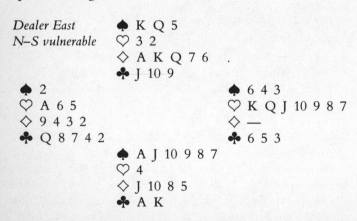

Dealer East
N–S vulnerable

```
                    ♠ K Q 5
                    ♡ 3 2
                    ♢ A K Q 7 6   .
                    ♣ J 10 9
  ♠ 2                                ♠ 6 4 3
  ♡ A 6 5                            ♡ K Q J 10 9 8 7
  ♢ 9 4 3 2                          ♢ —
  ♣ Q 8 7 4 2                        ♣ 6 5 3
                    ♠ A J 10 9 8 7
                    ♡ 4
                    ♢ J 10 8 5
                    ♣ A K
```

South	West	North	East
—	—	—	3♡
3♠	No	5♠	No
6♠	No	No	No

North had a rather awkward choice of bid over South's three spades. Would four diamonds be forcing? In theory, perhaps, but if South had stretched over three hearts he might hesitate to bid again. It is foolish to make delicate approaches when an opponent has pre-empted, so I approve of North's five spades.

When West leads the ace of hearts, which card should East play? He wants a diamond, obviously, but how will he indicate this?

The king of hearts would invite a heart. The 7 of hearts, the lowest card, would invite a switch to the low suit, clubs, and the queen of hearts would invite a diamond. If East were indifferent, or wanted partner to make the decision, he would play a middle card, such as the 9.

Mind you, there are other less ethical ways of indicating a preference. The story is told of a player who, like East in the diagram above, held no card lower than the 7 and did not trust his partner to recognize that the 7 (from 9 8 7) was meant to be a discouraging signal. Quite neatly, he dropped the 7 on the floor and made a business of picking it up. 'Sorry, I'm playing this one,' he said. 'What is it?' asked his partner. 'A low one.'

Tables turned by trials and tribulations

The Spingold Trophy, one of America's two premier knock-out team events, dates back to 1934. Since 1937 it has been the centre-piece of the Summer Nationals, and in recent years the winners have qualified for the trials to select the American team for the world championship.

There have been many memorable struggles, but none to match the drama of the 1984 Spingold; 119 teams entered, all with high qualifications. Six of the sixteen seeds failed to survive the first day's play and only four remained among the last sixteen.

But if there were shock results at the table, the real drama occurred elsewhere. Edith Rosenkranz, the wife of George Rosenkranz, captain of the third seeds, was kidnapped. Rosenkranz is a rich man (his company developed 'the Pill') and a substantial ransom was demanded; it was paid and happily Edith was released safely.

This horrifying story had a satisfactory ending. The police, displaying all the ingenuity that is attributed to them in television programmes, were somehow in touch with the kidnappers. They were soon arrested and the money was recovered. One of them was a Houston bridge player; he received a life sentence.

There was a further scandal of a familiar kind. A team withdrew from the competition after a meeting with the disciplinary committee. As usual, the affair reached an inconclusive ending.

Rosenkranz did not play on himself, but his team, the third seeds, progressed to the final, where they met the twelfth seed, Sontag. The 64-board match was closely

contested. When the last quarter began, Rosenkranz led by
23 IMPs. Almost half this lead disappeared on the first
board after the resumption:

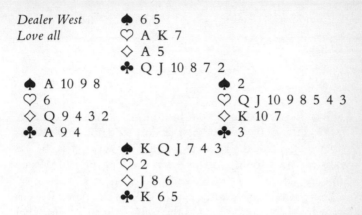

Dealer West　♠ 6 5
Love all　♡ A K 7
　♢ A 5
　♣ Q J 10 8 7 2

♠ A 10 9 8　　　　　　♠ 2
♡ 6　　　　　　　　　　♡ Q J 10 9 8 5 4 3
♢ Q 9 4 3 2　　　　　　♢ K 10 7
♣ A 9 4　　　　　　　　♣ 3

　♠ K Q J 7 4 3
　♡ 2
　♢ J 8 6
　♣ K 6 5

This was the bidding in the open rooms, where Sontag
was South:

South	West	North	East
—	1♢	2♣	4♡
4♠	dble	No	No
5♣	dble	No	No
No			

Some players would have refrained from doubling four
spades on the grounds that this suited them well, but there
is much to be said for the philosophy of doubling 'the bid
under your nose'. As it happens, five clubs is as vulnerable
as four spades. A spade lead and ruff, followed by a
diamond switch, brings in 300.

However, East led a spade and West tried for the
shadow rather than the substance by switching to his
singleton heart. North won and led the jack of clubs. Now
it was too late for the defence to make a trick in diamonds.

The declarer could ruff a heart with the king of clubs and discard his losing diamond on dummy's spades.

That was 550 to Sontag. At the other table:

South	West	North	East
—	No	2♣	4♡
4♠	dble	No	5♡
No	No	dble	No
No	No		

Here East's take-out into five hearts seems untrusting. As a rule, a player who has pre-empted should allow his partner to make the next decision. However, five hearts was only one down, so there was a swing of 10 IMPs to Sontag.

There was more drama before the finish. After Rosenkranz had been announced as the winner, it was found that there had been a misboarding near the end. At about 4 a.m. the deal was replayed – in so mysterious a manner that even the officials were able to judge that something was rotten in the State of Denmark. It was. The players at one table knew, though the tournament director did not, that if there was a misboarding near the finish the deal had to be cancelled, not replayed.

19

Mixed result for transatlantic partnership

American visitors, if not among the top players, are regarded as something of a hazard at my club. They play old-fashioned Goren and it is prudent to ask whether they are used to a conventional two-club opening. If you open 1NT they expect you to hold the earth, and once the bidding has attained a certain impetus it is impossible to keep them in check. Except that it turned out well, I had a typical experience on this deal:

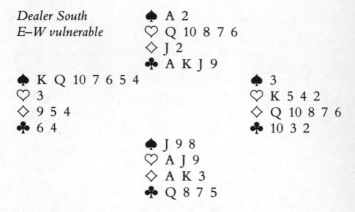

Dealer South
E–W vulnerable

♠ A 2
♡ Q 10 8 7 6
◇ J 2
♣ A K J 9

♠ K Q 10 7 6 5 4
♡ 3
◇ 9 5 4
♣ 6 4

♠ 3
♡ K 5 4 2
◇ Q 10 8 7 6
♣ 10 3 2

♠ J 9 8
♡ A J 9
◇ A K 3
♣ Q 8 7 5

Sitting South, I opened 1NT, guiltily aware that I was under strength according to my partner's methods. West overcalled with two spades and after various gyrations, too hideous to relate, we ended in 6NT. 'Guess I'll let you play this one,' said my partner expansively, as he spread the dummy.

I captured the spade lead with the ace and ran the 10 of

hearts successfully. West showed out on the next round, but it wasn't fatal. After the ace of hearts and three rounds of clubs the position was:

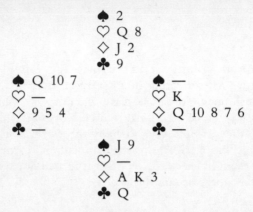

♠ 2
♡ Q 8
♢ J 2
♣ 9

♠ Q 10 7   ♠ —
♡ —   ♡ K
♢ 9 5 4   ♢ Q 10 8 7 6
♣ —   ♣ —

♠ J 9
♡ —
♢ A K 3
♣ Q

East was thrown in with the ♡ K and I let his diamond run to the jack.

There was a point in the play which you may not have noticed. South must not make the mistake of cashing the fourth round of clubs. If he does this, then the return of the queen of diamonds by East is a killing defence.

We have a merciful rule at the club that the same partners cannot cut together in successive rubbers, but later in the afternoon we found ourselves in the East–West positions. My partner was East and this is what he could see:

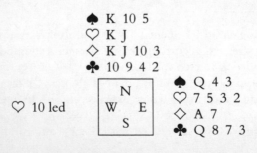

♠ K 10 5
♡ K J
♢ K J 10 3
♣ 10 9 4 2

	N	
W		E
	S	

♡ 10 led

♠ Q 4 3
♡ 7 5 3 2
♢ A 7
♣ Q 8 7 3

64

South was in four spades and I led the 10 of hearts. South overtook the jack with the queen and ran the 9 of spades to East's queen. What should East play now?

My partner returned a low club. Not a success, because the full hand was:

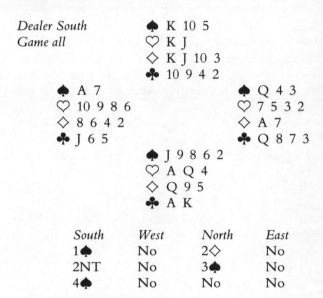

Dealer South
Game all

♠ K 10 5
♡ K J
♢ K J 10 3
♣ 10 9 4 2

♠ A 7
♡ 10 9 8 6
♢ 8 6 4 2
♣ J 6 5

♠ Q 4 3
♡ 7 5 3 2
♢ A 7
♣ Q 8 7 3

♠ J 9 8 6 2
♡ A Q 4
♢ Q 9 5
♣ A K

South	West	North	East
1♠	No	2♢	No
2NT	No	3♣	No
4♠	No	No	No

South, you will recall, won the heart lead and ran the 9 of spades to East's queen. East returned a club and South lost only to the two aces.

'Nothing to be done about that,' East remarked, as we added up the score.

'You might,' I suggested, 'have played the ace and another diamond when you were in. Then we get a diamond ruff.'

He seemed to think that this would have been a flight of unreasonable fancy. Of course, when declarer finessed on the first round of trumps, it was obvious that he did not hold the ace.

20

Don't throw away your defence

Everyone agrees that defence is the most difficult part of the game, and perhaps discarding is the most difficult part of defence. Finding a series of discards can be as daunting for the expert as for the novice, because not only must a defender keep the right cards, but often he must do so without allowing the declarer to notice his discomfort. Small considerations of this kind are not prominent in an amateur game. Here is an everyday sort of muddle:

```
Dealer South        ♠ 10 8 6 5
N–S vulnerable      ♡ A 7 6 4
                    ◇ K J 6 2
                    ♣ 4
♠ K 9 3                              ♠ J 4 2
♡ 10                                 ♡ Q 8 2
◇ A 10 8 4                           ◇ Q 7 5
♣ A 9 8 7 3                          ♣ K 10 6 2
                    ♠ A Q 7
                    ♡ K J 9 5 3
                    ◇ 9 3
                    ♣ Q J 5
```

South	West	North	East
1♡	dble	3♡	No
4♡	No	No	No

South's bid of four hearts was unsound, of course, but perhaps he had played against these two opponents before.

A singleton trump is normally not considered a good

lead, because it tends to cost when partner has a holding such as Q x x or K J x x. This objection does not apply when the leader has made a take-out double, because this already marks him with a shortage. So there was nothing wrong here with West's lead of ♡ 10.

South played well by disdaining the free finesse. He went up with dummy's ace of hearts and advanced the singleton club. East, not unreasonably, went in with the king of clubs to lead a second trump. South finessed, according to plan, and West discarded a club. The next move was a diamond to the king and a second diamond, on which East went up with the queen to play a third round of trumps. This time West discarded a spade, leaving:

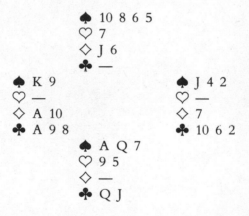

The queen of clubs was covered and ruffed, then a finesse of the ♠ Q lost to the king. It looks natural for West to play another club now, but he preferred the ace of diamonds, to clarify the position in this suit. With little to play for, South cashed his last trump, West throwing a diamond and dummy a spade. To West's horror, East detached first one card, then another, and finally the 4 of spades. 'As you doubled on very little, I thought you'd have four spades,' he explained to his partner.

67

I don't say it's a particularly interesting hand, but it is typical of what happens all the time at rubber bridge. East should have thought along these lines: 'If South had been 2–5–2–4 he would have played on clubs earlier, because of the entry situation. After the ♡ J the play would have been: the ♣ Q covered and ruffed, a spade to the ace, the jack and another club.'

The next hand was rather more difficult for East:

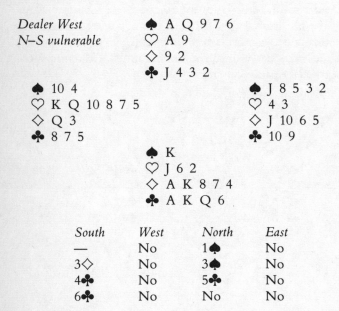

Dealer West
N–S vulnerable

♠ A Q 9 7 6
♡ A 9
♢ 9 2
♣ J 4 3 2

♠ 10 4
♡ K Q 10 8 7 5
♢ Q 3
♣ 8 7 5

♠ J 8 5 3 2
♡ 4 3
♢ J 10 6 5
♣ 10 9

♠ K
♡ J 6 2
♢ A K 8 7 4
♣ A K Q 6

South	West	North	East
—	No	1♠	No
3♢	No	3♠	No
4♣	No	5♣	No
6♣	No	No	No

The king of hearts was taken by the ace and two rounds of trumps were drawn by the ace and king. The best play now is to cash the king of spades, then play three rounds of diamonds, discarding dummy's heart if West follows suit.

At the table South made the rather poor play of drawing a third trump. East now faced an awkward discard. 'It looks as though South has K x of spades,' he thought. 'If I throw a heart now, he will cash the king of spades, then

68

play three rounds of diamonds, discarding dummy's heart and putting me on play. I think I must play partner for the king of diamonds.'

Having reached this conclusion, East discarded a diamond, which was clearly fatal. He could have postponed the decision by discarding a heart on the third club. Apart from that, his analysis was faulty because it placed West with seven hearts (declarer being 2–2–5–4), and with seven hearts to the K Q West would have opened three hearts.

There is almost always an answer, or at least an indication, when these problems arise. Don't play a card until you are satisfied that you have analysed all the possibilities.

21

This goes down in the agony column

A competitor in the European Championship may make one or two errors in a match that is easily won and not much reported, or he may be unlucky and miss the winning play when everyone is watching. This happened twice to Barnet Shenkin during the 1985 championship at Salsomaggiore. This was the first occasion, against Sweden:

Dealer West
Love all

```
                    ♠ Q 9 4 3
                    ♡ A K 8 6
                    ◇ J 10 8 4 3
                    ♣ —
  ♠ A K J 8 2                       ♠ 7 6 5
  ♡ 4 2                             ♡ Q J 10 7
  ◇ Q                               ◇ A K 7 6 5
  ♣ K 8 6 5 2                       ♣ 10
                    ♠ 10
                    ♡ 9 5 3
                    ◇ 9 2
                    ♣ A Q J 9 7 4 3
```

With Shenkin West and Coyle East, the bidding went:

South	West	North	East
—	1♠	No	2◇
3♣	dble	No	No
No			

West led the ace of spades, followed by the queen of diamonds, which was allowed to hold. As it was certain that he would have to lead spades again sooner or later, Barnet pressed on with the king of spades, ruffed by declarer. South cashed the ace of clubs and ace of hearts, discarded a heart on the queen of spades, and ruffed a spade. After a heart to the king the position was:

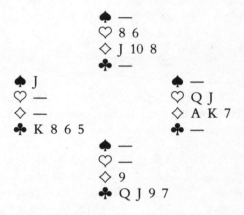

A heart was ruffed with the queen of clubs and West discarded a spade. South led a diamond; West had to ruff and made only one more trick; 470 to Sweden.

Well played by Gothe, but Shenkin had a chance. Did you spot it? When the heart is ruffed by the queen of clubs he must underruff! Then a diamond goes to East and on the next trick West underruffs again, making the K 8 of clubs at the finish. At the other table the bidding was the same, but the declarer did not follow the same line and was always going one down.

The most you can say of that deal is that Barnet missed a chance for the Brilliancy prize. You could say the same again about this hand from the match against Austria:

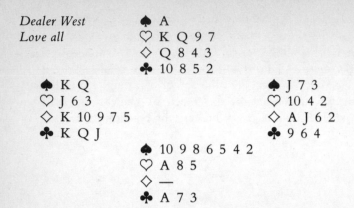

Dealer West
Love all

	♠ A
	♡ K Q 9 7
	◇ Q 8 4 3
	♣ 10 8 5 2

♠ K Q		♠ J 7 3
♡ J 6 3		♡ 10 4 2
◇ K 10 9 7 5		◇ A J 6 2
♣ K Q J		♣ 9 6 4

	♠ 10 9 8 6 5 4 2
	♡ A 8 5
	◇ —
	♣ A 7 3

In the closed room the Austrians scrambled nine tricks in three hearts. In the open room Shenkin was South and there was a spirited auction:

South	West	North	East
—	1◇	1♡	No
1♠	No	No	1NT
3♣	3NT	dble	redble
No	4◇	No	No
4♡	No	4♠	No
No	No		

South won the second club, crossed to the ace of spades, and ruffed a diamond. Then he led the 10 of spades, hoping that whoever won this trick would not have a club to play. Unlucky, one down.

Do you think you would have made this contract? Are you sure you can make it now, with all the cards exposed?

Try winning the *first* club, cross to the ace of spades, and discard a club on the fourth heart. Whether West or East ruffs, the defenders make just a club and one more spade. The difficult part about this is that if South holds off the first club and wins the second, West will discard his last

72

club when the heart is ruffed, and then the defenders will make two more trump tricks.

The winning play on this deal is known in France as the *coup d'agonie*. I wonder what they call it in Glasgow.

22

It can be different at the table

Most of the bridge magazines conduct a competition in which tricky questions of bidding are answered by readers and later by a panel of experts. If well done, these features are both interesting and instructive. I came across this problem in a French magazine. East–West are vulnerable and the bidding goes:

South	West	North	East
—	—	3♠	No
No	3NT	No	4♡
?			

Sitting South, you hold:

♠ 9
♡ 10 9 8
♢ A Q J 10 9 6
♣ A 3 2

Certainly it would be a mistake to bid five diamonds, so the choice is between pass and double. On balance, it seems right to pass. If partner has the ace of spades you will put them one down, but if not they may make an overtrick. Mathematically, the odds do not favour close doubles. The majority of the experts took this view.

I had a feeling that I had seen the hand before, and indeed it occurred during a South American championship.

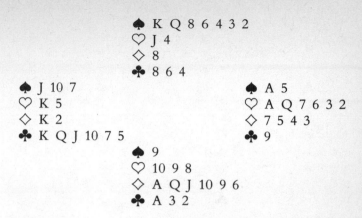

♠ K Q 8 6 4 3 2
♥ J 4
♦ 8
♣ 8 6 4

♠ J 10 7
♥ K 5
♦ K 2
♣ K Q J 10 7 5

♠ A 5
♥ A Q 7 6 3 2
♦ 7 5 4 3
♣ 9

♠ 9
♥ 10 9 8
♦ A Q J 10 9 6
♣ A 3 2

Screens were in use, but you can generally tell who has been taking time, and the Venezuelan South noted that East had thought for a long while before bidding four hearts. It seemed clear that East was uncertain about the meaning of his partner's 3NT. Was it 'unusual', asking for the minors, or was it natural?

To give his opponents a push in the wrong direction, South doubled four hearts. East now changed his mind and bid five diamonds, which went four down. And East–West were not greenhorns – they were the celebrated Brazilian partnership of Chagas and Assumpçao!

The same players were hardly the heroes of this deal from the Pairs Olympiad at New Orleans – but their reputations will survive it.

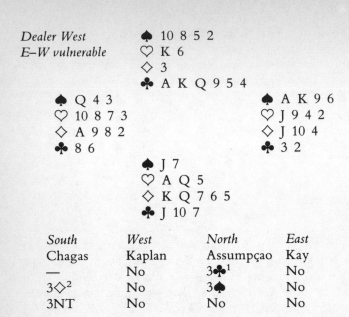

Dealer West
E–W vulnerable

♠ 10 8 5 2
♡ K 6
♢ 3
♣ A K Q 9 5 4

♠ Q 4 3   ♠ A K 9 6
♡ 10 8 7 3   ♡ J 9 4 2
♢ A 9 8 2   ♢ J 10 4
♣ 8 6   ♣ 3 2

♠ J 7
♡ A Q 5
♢ K Q 7 6 5
♣ J 10 7

South	West	North	East
Chagas	Kaplan	Assumpçao	Kay
—	No	3♣[1]	No
3♢[2]	No	3♠	No
3NT	No	No	No

[1] They were playing a one-club system, so the opening bid promised just good clubs with an outside trick.

[2] This, probably, was a relay asking for further information.

West led the 8 of hearts (second best from a moderate suit) and South won in dummy. What should he play next, do you think? Playing pairs, and hoping to snatch an overtrick before the opponents knew what was happening, the declarer led a diamond from dummy at trick two. Unlucky! West won and switched to a low spade. Now the defenders took four tricks in this suit.

Overtricks are important in pairs play, so was Chagas right to try the diamond at trick two? It is fairly certain that if East had held the diamond ace he would have won the trick and led a heart, not a spade. Even as things were, the defenders had to play particularly well to take four spade tricks in a hurry.

Still, my own feeling is that it would have been better play for South to run the six club tricks. One of my first partners was the great British player, Maurice Harrison-Gray, and it was always his style to play off winners and see what happened. Discarding at the table is far more difficult than when all the cards are visible in a diagram.

23

Cold chill strikes heart

When one good player says of another that he is 'difficult to play against', it is a considerable, if grudging, compliment. The declarer had a problem on this first hand, but by disguising it he caused an opponent to make a mistake.

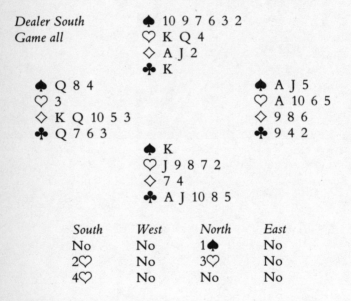

Dealer South
Game all

	♠ 10 9 7 6 3 2	
	♡ K Q 4	
	◇ A J 2	
	♣ K	

♠ Q 8 4		♠ A J 5
♡ 3		♡ A 10 6 5
◇ K Q 10 5 3		◇ 9 8 6
♣ Q 7 6 3		♣ 9 4 2

	♠ K	
	♡ J 9 8 7 2	
	◇ 7 4	
	♣ A J 10 8 5	

South	West	North	East
No	No	1♠	No
2♡	No	3♡	No
4♡	No	No	No

South won the diamond lead in dummy, cashed the king of clubs, and led the 6 of spades from the table. East went in with the ace and returned a diamond to his partner's queen. West now switched to a trump. East won with the ace and played a second round to dummy's queen.

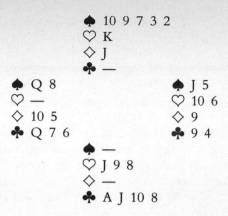

♠ 10 9 7 3 2
♡ K
♢ J
♣ —

♠ Q 8
♡ —
♢ 10 5
♣ Q 7 6

♠ J 5
♡ 10 6
♢ 9
♣ 9 4

♠ —
♡ J 9 8
♢ —
♣ A J 10 8

South needs the rest and, as you can see, his prospects are not good. Playing with a steady tempo, he cashed the jack of diamonds, ruffed a spade, and led the 10 of clubs. West, not there, played low. Now South cashed the ace of clubs, ruffed a club with the king of hearts, and was happily in dummy at trick 12. If South had cashed the ace of clubs earlier, it would have been much easier for West to cover with the queen on the next round.

On the next deal North–South reached a dubious grand slam against strong opposition.

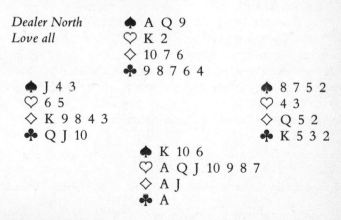

Dealer North
Love all

♠ A Q 9
♡ K 2
♢ 10 7 6
♣ 9 8 7 6 4

♠ J 4 3
♡ 6 5
♢ K 9 8 4 3
♣ Q J 10

♠ 8 7 5 2
♡ 4 3
♢ Q 5 2
♣ K 5 3 2

♠ K 10 6
♡ A Q J 10 9 8 7
♢ A J
♣ A

South	West	North	East
—	—	No	No
2♡	No	3♡[1]	No
4♣	No	4♡	No
4♠	No	5♠[2]	No
7♡[3]	No	No	No

[1] The immediate raise, for most Acol players, promises trump support and an ace. It was the best bid here.

[2] He has signed off once and is being pushed to declare any additional values.

[3] 'I could count 12 tricks on top,' South said afterwards. It is true that these hands with a long suit often produce an extra trick.

West led the queen of clubs to South's ace. The declarer drew a round of trumps, then led the 6 of spades. West played the 3 and . . .

Are you sure you might not have made the same mistake as West? South, who had played at normal pace so far, now checked his calculations, and a cold chill struck West's heart. Having confirmed that he would need the extra entry, South finessed the 9 of spades and in time established the fifth club for a diamond discard.

'The fact that I had led a club made the defence more difficult,' West remarked to me later. 'If I had led a trump, for example, and South had cashed the ace of clubs before leading a low spade, I would have realized what was happening.' He meant, of course, that he would have played the jack of spades on the first round, to prevent the declarer from gaining three spade entries to dummy.

24

Dark lady of fortune

The declarer's problem on this first hand was to recognize the slight chance that existed.

Dealer South　　　　♠ Q 9 8
Game all　　　　　　♡ 7 2
　　　　　　　　　　♢ Q J 8 7 4
　　　　　　　　　　♣ A K 3

♠ K 10 6 5　　　　　　　　　　　♠ J 7 3 2
♡ A K Q J 10 9　　　　　　　　♡ 6 5 4
♢ 2　　　　　　　　　　　　　　♢ 6 5
♣ Q 8　　　　　　　　　　　　　♣ J 10 7 2

　　　　　　　　　　♠ A 4
　　　　　　　　　　♡ 8 3
　　　　　　　　　　♢ A K 10 9 3
　　　　　　　　　　♣ 9 6 5 4

In a preliminary round of Crockford's Cup the bidding went:

South	West	North	East
No	1♡	No	No
2♢	3♡	4♢	No
No	No		

Most players, certainly, would have opened the bidding on South's hand, but his length was in the minor suits and the pass was quite sensible. (South did open at the other table and lost points in five diamonds.)

Defending against four diamonds, West cashed two

hearts and exited with a trump. South played a club to the ace and immediately returned a low club. When West won with the queen he was end-played.

This was neat play by the declarer. Had he come back to hand with a second round of diamonds he would have given West a chance to throw the queen of clubs. West, of course, should have played the queen of clubs on the first round of the suit, but not many players would have done so.

The dark lady was – or might have been – a critical card on this deal from a friendly match between Britain and Italy:

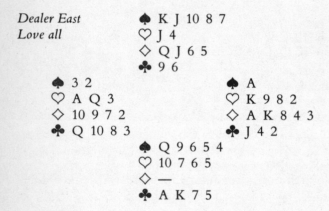

Dealer East
Love all

♠ K J 10 8 7
♡ J 4
♢ Q J 6 5
♣ 9 6

♠ 3 2
♡ A Q 3
♢ 10 9 7 2
♣ Q 10 8 3

♠ A
♡ K 9 8 2
♢ A K 8 4 3
♣ J 4 2

♠ Q 9 6 5 4
♡ 10 7 6 5
♢ —
♣ A K 7 5

Consider South's prospects in four spades. There are only three top losers, but to succeed in the contract South needs to ruff two losers in hearts and two in clubs. The defenders can prevent this if they contrive to play two rounds of trumps early on. The Italian East–West failed to do this, so the British declarer made the game.

At the other table the bidding went:

South	West	North	East
Mariano	Rose	Di Stefano	Sheehan
—	—	—	1◇
1♠	dble[1]	3♠	4♡[2]
4♠	dble[3]	No	No
No			

[1] The negative double of one spade normally promises four hearts. The alternative was a simple raise to two diamonds.

[2] Expecting his partner to hold four hearts.

[3] 'I doubled to stop you going on,' is usually the cry of the moderate players who don't trust their partners. Here the situation is a little different, because West has misled his partner to some extent. At all costs he must dissuade East from bidding on.

Mariano covered the 10 of diamonds with the jack and ruffed the king. Preparing for a cross-ruff, he led a low heart. West went in with the queen and led a trump to his partner's ace. Sheehan returned a heart and a second round of trumps defeated the contract.

'I was hoping you'd play a club when you were in with the ace of spades,' South remarked to East. 'Then I play ace, king and another club, discarding the second heart from dummy. You have no more trumps, so I make the rest on a cross-ruff.'

'Not necessarily,' said Rose. 'If you play that way I go up with the queen of clubs on the third round, so that you can't duck the trick to my partner.'

As you see, the queen of clubs played a fateful role – or might have done – on both hands. On the first it was a liability, on the second a life-saver.

25

Eight top spades not mentioned

'How could I tell?' is the melancholy cry after many
disasters at the bridge table. Well, there's almost always an
answer. On this occasion neither defender used his head.

```
Dealer East        ♠ A K Q 10 8 7 6 5
Love all           ♡ 4
                   ◇ 9 2
                   ♣ Q 5
♠ —                                    ♠ 9 4 3 2
♡ A 7 2                                ♡ Q 3
◇ K J 8 4 3                            ◇ 10 7 5
♣ 10 8 7 6 3                          ♣ A J 9 2
                   ♠ J
                   ♡ K J 10 9 8 6 5
                   ◇ A Q 6
                   ♣ K 4
```

South	West	North	East
—	—	—	No
4♡[1]	No	No[2]	No

[1] At rubber bridge, anyway, it is sensible to pre-empt
    occasionally on fairly strong hands.. This is especially
    true when your suit is hearts, not spades.
[2] The textbooks that mention this sequence say that a
    game call in a major suit over a pre-empt is not forcing.
    It may be that North didn't altogether trust his partner
    to pass four spades.

West led a low diamond to the 10 and queen. South's first move was a low club to the queen; if this had held he would probably have taken the diamond ruff and then tried to discard his second club on a spade. When East won with the ace of clubs he returned a trump. South, for no very good reason that I can see, tried the king. After West had taken this trick the position was:

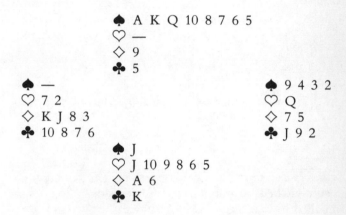

A diamond seems natural now, but West led a club to the jack and king. East won the next trick with the queen of hearts and the defence had yet another chance. East fingered a spade, put it back, and returned a club; ten tricks made instead of eight.

'If you'd led the king of diamonds when you were in I would have realized you wanted a spade,' said East.

That was a fair point, but East's own play was far worse. There were two sure indications: if South had been void in spades he would have played for a diamond ruff, then led a spade from dummy; and if West had begun with a singleton spade and A x or A x x of the trump suit, he would surely have led the singleton.

The defence on this deal was more difficult:

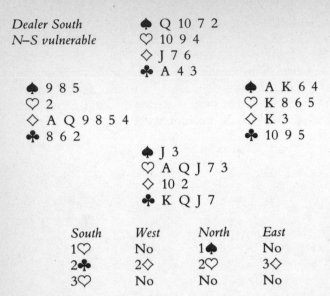

Dealer South
N–S vulnerable

North
♠ Q 10 7 2
♡ 10 9 4
◇ J 7 6
♣ A 4 3

West
♠ 9 8 5
♡ 2
◇ A Q 9 8 5 4
♣ 8 6 2

East
♠ A K 6 4
♡ K 8 6 5
◇ K 3
♣ 10 9 5

South
♠ J 3
♡ A Q J 7 3
◇ 10 2
♣ K Q J 7

South	West	North	East
1♡	No	1♠	No
2♣	2◇	2♡	3◇
3♡	No	No	No

West's lead of the 9 of spades was taken by the king, and East switched to the king of diamonds. When West signalled in diamonds East continued the suit and South ruffed the third round, East discarding a club. South crossed to the ♣ A and played the 10 of hearts, followed by a heart to the queen, on which West showed out. This left:

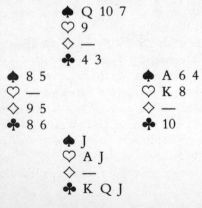

♠ Q 10 7
♡ 9
◇ —
♣ 4 3

♠ 8 5
♡ —
◇ 9 5
♣ 8 6

♠ A 6 4
♡ K 8
◇ —
♣ 10

♠ J
♡ A J
◇ —
♣ K Q J

Gauging the distribution well, South cashed one high club, then overtook the ♠ J with the ♠ Q. East could only return a spade and after cashing two tricks South was left in dummy at trick 12.

Not easy to see in time, but after the king of diamonds East should have cashed the other spade winner. The defence follows with two rounds of diamonds, forcing South to ruff, and eventually East will make a trump trick.

26

Sometimes, at pairs, the wrong play is right

You will sometimes hear people dismiss pairs contests, with their emphasis on overtricks, as an unnatural, artificial form of bridge. But is rubber-bridge scoring, with the divisions between three spades and four spades, four diamonds and five diamonds, *natural*? Not really, we are just used to it. The play in a pairs event is undoubtedly keener, affording more opportunities than rubber bridge.

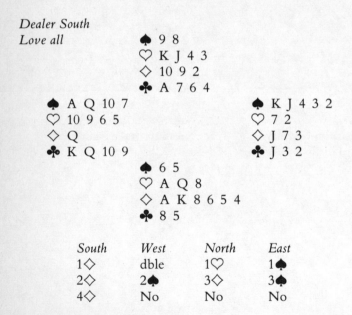

Dealer South
Love all

		♠ 9 8		
		♡ K J 4 3		
		♢ 10 9 2		
		♣ A 7 6 4		

♠ A Q 10 7		♠ K J 4 3 2
♡ 10 9 6 5		♡ 7 2
♢ Q		♢ J 7 3
♣ K Q 10 9		♣ J 3 2

	♠ 6 5
	♡ A Q 8
	♢ A K 8 6 5 4
	♣ 8 5

South	West	North	East
1♢	dble	1♡	1♠
2♢	2♠	3♢	3♠
4♢	No	No	No

There were several aggressive bids in this auction, characteristic of pairs play. West's raise to two spades is doubtful after a minimum double, and South, at rubber bridge, might pass over three spades.

West leads the king of clubs; South wins in dummy and plays a diamond to the ace, on which the queen drops. Considering this suit on its own, the finesse is a better chance than playing for the drop; it is fair to reflect that with Q J West might have dropped the jack, not the queen. Furthermore, East–West possess limited values and the fact that they have bid as high as three spades certainly suggests that the diamonds are 3–1 rather than 2–2. A declarer at rubber bridge would take these two points into consideration and would cross to dummy with a heart, then take the diamond finesse.

This is the winning line as the cards lie, but in a pairs event you have to ask yourself what is happening at other tables. Since your four diamonds was borderline, some East–West pairs may play in three spades. If the hearts are 4–2 and the diamonds 3–1 they will make it. In this case you won't do badly to play in four diamonds and lose 50. So you may decide to cash the ace and king of diamonds, and then play on hearts. You go one down, but it won't be fatal. What *would* be fatal would be to lose points in four diamonds when East-West could not make three spades.

This is another hand where the declarer has to apply the same kind of reasoning:

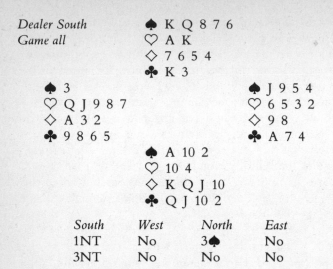

Dealer South
Game all

♠ K Q 8 7 6
♡ A K
♢ 7 6 5 4
♣ K 3

♠ 3
♡ Q J 9 8 7
♢ A 3 2
♣ 9 8 6 5

♠ J 9 5 4
♡ 6 5 3 2
♢ 9 8
♣ A 7 4

♠ A 10 2
♡ 10 4
♢ K Q J 10
♣ Q J 10 2

South	West	North	East
1NT	No	3♠	No
3NT	No	No	No

I am far from commending South's 3NT on this occasion, but it is worth remarking that 3NT is often made when there is 'no play for it'.

Whatever South's reasons may have been, he cannot have been happy when a heart was led. Oh yes, 3NT will be easy if the spades break, but ten tricks at notrumps will be the limit, while everyone else (still assuming the spade break) will be making eleven.

In South's position, what would you do? You might, against some opposition, try to slip a low club to the jack at trick two; then you would be in line for eleven tricks at notrumps. But few opponents, seeing the lone A K of hearts on the table, would fail to go in quickly with the ace of clubs and clear partner's suit.

Then has South *any* chance of a fair score? Yes, there is just one hope: assume that the spades break badly and base your play on that possibility. In other words, lead a low spade to the 10 at trick two. If this leads to ten tricks at notrumps, instead of just ten tricks in spades, you can annoy the opposition by telling them to hold their cards up!

27

Tiger in a cage

Players often ask why British teams are not so successful at championship level as they used to be. There are two reasons, really: the most important is that the all-round standard has improved enormously, the other that the artificial systems, now played by several teams, are levellers. The committees who decide these matters make a great parade of insisting that all countries should submit detailed accounts of the methods played by all their pairs. This makes almost no difference, because when one is playing at the table for seven or eight hours a day one has no time or energy to study the methods of the next opponents; and even if this is done, many unfamiliar and unexplained sequences will occur.

The game was easier when I first played in international events. Of the stronger teams, only the Italians played an unfamiliar system, and we had time to study the Blue Club and the Roman Club. We also had a countermeasure, the Little Major system.

The semifinal of the 1964 Olympiad was a dramatic occasion. Though we lost in the end, we had the better of the luck on two big hands. This was one of them:

Dealer North
Game all

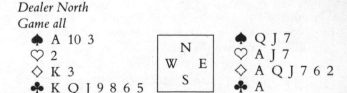

	♠ A 10 3		♠ Q J 7
	♡ 2		♡ A J 7
	◇ K 3		◇ A Q J 7 6 2
	♣ K Q J 9 8 6 5		♣ A

The bidding at one table went:

South	West	North	East
Garozzo	Harrison-Gray	Forquet	Flint
—	—	No	2NT[1]
No	4♣[2]	No	4NT
No	7NT	No	No
No			

[1] Not everyone's choice, I realize.

2 Asking for aces.

At the other table Avarelli and Belladonna played in seven diamonds. Unlucky, the spades were 7–0 and the spade lead was ruffed.

With 20 boards to go, we were 15 behind. Then we had another stroke of luck when Reese and Schapiro held:

♠ Q 8 3		♠ A K 6 5 4
♡ 7 4 3	N	♡ A K 9 6 5 2
◇ A 9 6 4	W E	◇ 7
♣ K Q 4	S	♣ A

This was the bidding in the Little Major system:

West	East
Schapiro	Reese
—	1◇[1]
2◇	3♡
4♡[2]	4NT
5◇	6♣[3]
7♡[4]	

1 This showed either a spade suit or a strong notrump.

2 East was marked with a major two-suiter, the hearts probably longer than the spades.

3 Seeking reassurance about the quality of West's trumps.

4 Schapiro, who played the system with all the relish of a tiger confined in a cage, treated six clubs as a generalized grand-slam try.

Lucky again, the trumps breaking 2–2. And this was the final board, with Italy leading by 11 IMPs:

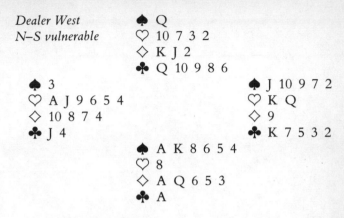

Dealer West
N–S vulnerable

♠ Q
♡ 10 7 3 2
♢ K J 2
♣ Q 10 9 8 6

♠ 3
♡ A J 9 6 5 4
♢ 10 8 7 4
♣ J 4

♠ J 10 9 7 2
♡ K Q
♢ 9
♣ K 7 5 3 2

♠ A K 8 6 5 4
♡ 8
♢ A Q 6 5 3
♣ A

Avarelli and Belladonna, playing the Roman system, bid to six diamonds. It was a reasonable contract, but after a heart lead and continuation Avarelli was three down. If Gray and Konstam, two superb match players, could make a game at the other table, Britain would win the match. This was the bidding:

South	West	North	East
Harrison-Gray	Forquet	Konstam	Garozzo
—	2♡[1]	No	No
3♡[2]	No	5♣[3]	No
5♠	No	No	No

[1] Early days for a weak two bid.
[2] Intending to convert a club response to spades, showing diamonds by inference.
[3] This bid was criticized on the grounds that four clubs would have been forcing. But with the queen of spades and K J x of diamonds, all vital cards, would North then have passed over partner's four spades? I doubt it.

Gray played the hand with great skill and was only one down. We lost the match by 8 points and Italy won the final.

Sometimes show distribution,
sometimes show sense

Piqued by the suggestion that most of their decisions were reached in the bar, the selectors on one occasion persuaded me to watch the proceedings in a junior international trial. This was the first hand I observed:

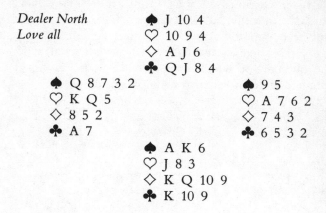

Dealer North
Love all

```
              ♠ J 10 4
              ♡ 10 9 4
              ◇ A J 6
              ♣ Q J 8 4
♠ Q 8 7 3 2                      ♠ 9 5
♡ K Q 5                          ♡ A 7 6 2
◇ 8 5 2                          ◇ 7 4 3
♣ A 7                            ♣ 6 5 3 2
              ♠ A K 6
              ♡ J 8 3
              ◇ K Q 10 9
              ♣ K 10 9
```

It wasn't easy, even for modern players, to avoid a final contract of 3NT. Three suits were named, but none of them, it seemed, was natural. West led the 3 of spades. The defenders, obviously, can take four hearts and a club, but the play is not so easy.

South won the spade lead in dummy and advanced the 10 of hearts – an ancient ruse to discourage opponents from attacking this suit. It worked well because East, quite naturally, went up with the ace of hearts to lead a second spade. This might well have been the correct play, but unfortunately the hearts were now blocked.

Later I watched this board at another table. The contract was the same, but South employed a different stratagem. He played the jack of spades from dummy at trick one and overtook with the king. Then he led the king of clubs. West won and, thinking that South held ♣ A K alone, led a second spade. South now made ten tricks.

'What did you make of my 9 of spades?' East demanded. 'I was showing you a doubleton. I wouldn't have played the 9 from 9 x x.'

This was true, and I think West was at fault. He maintained that the 9 was an encouraging card, showing that a spade continuation was recommended. However, the usual convention nowadays, when the third player cannot head dummy's card, is to show length, playing high-low from an even number.

The question of whether or not it is wise to signal distribution in defence arose on another deal:

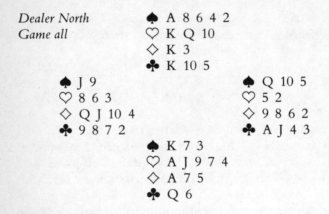

Dealer North
Game all

```
              ♠ A 8 6 4 2
              ♡ K Q 10
              ◇ K 3
              ♣ K 10 5
♠ J 9                        ♠ Q 10 5
♡ 8 6 3                      ♡ 5 2
◇ Q J 10 4                   ◇ 9 8 6 2
♣ 9 8 7 2                    ♣ A J 4 3
              ♠ K 7 3
              ♡ A J 9 7 4
              ◇ A 7 5
              ♣ Q 6
```

It was difficult, on the values held, to stop short of a slam. The bidding went:

South	West	North	East
—	—	1♠	No
2♡	No	4♡	No
6♡	No	No	No

I agree with South's jump to six hearts. There were gaps in the spades and hearts, and to bid 4NT or five diamonds might assist the defenders to find the best lead.

The hands did not fit well in the sense that there was an apparent loser in spades, but a diamond ruff, plus a successful finesse of the 10 of clubs, would provide a parking-place for declarer's third spade. South won the diamond lead and played a low club from dummy. East played low and the queen won. South cashed the ◇ A, ruffed the third round, and drew trumps.

The defenders, meanwhile, had dutifully signalled in a way that suggested even numbers in both diamonds and clubs. If these suits were breaking 4–4, then East would hold three spades. Changing his tactics, South played a fourth trump, reaching this position:

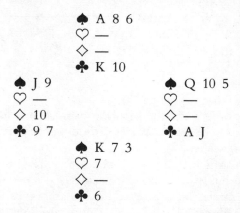

A spade was thrown from dummy on the fifth trump and East was squeezed.

97

29

Time to put the armchair critics on trial

Bridge, like golf and many other games, is easier to play from the analyst's armchair than on the course. But even with the benefit of hindsight and a look at all four hands, the critics' comments are often unjust.

This was board 18 of a World Olympiad match between the women's teams of Britain and the United States:

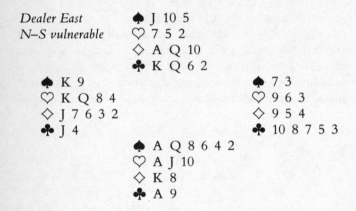

Dealer East
N–S vulnerable

North:
♠ J 10 5
♡ 7 5 2
♢ A Q 10
♣ K Q 6 2

West:
♠ K 9
♡ K Q 8 4
♢ J 7 6 3 2
♣ J 4

East:
♠ 7 3
♡ 9 6 3
♢ 9 5 4
♣ 10 8 7 5 3

South:
♠ A Q 8 6 4 2
♡ A J 10
♢ K 8
♣ A 9

In the open room the British pair finished in 6NT. They had no chance when West led the king of hearts and the spade finesse failed.

Jacqui Mitchell and Gail Moss, for the United States, reached six spades. This, evidently, is a better contract because, even on a heart lead, declarer may reasonably hope to discard her hearts on dummy's winners in the minor suits.

Sandra Landy (West) led the king of hearts and Moss

won. Three rounds of diamonds provided one heart discard, but the third round of clubs was ruffed, while declarer disposed of her last heart. 'Surprisingly,' the official bulletin commented, 'West continued with a diamond, giving Moss a useless ruff-and-discard. But why, Moss wondered, did West play a diamond instead of the more likely heart? Perhaps West was hoping for an uppercut of some sort to promote a trump trick. But what trump could West possibly have? Only the king. So Moss played the ace of spades, felling the king and making the slam.'

This was good play by Moss, but also good play by the defender. Clearly, if West does not present the declarer with a ruff-and-discard, she will never make a trick with the king of spades, since dummy has no entry for a finesse.

One other point: do you think that it would have been better play by South to cash the ace of spades before playing for discards on the minor suits? This would gain if West held a singleton spade and a doubleton club.

The next accused is the American player, Bob Hamman. I am going to urge you to find my client not guilty. At worst, you may return a verdict of not proven.

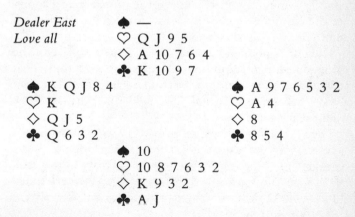

```
Dealer East      ♠ —
Love all         ♡ Q J 9 5
                 ◇ A 10 7 6 4
                 ♣ K 10 9 7
♠ K Q J 8 4              ♠ A 9 7 6 5 3 2
♡ K                      ♡ A 4
◇ Q J 5                  ◇ 8
♣ Q 6 3 2                ♣ 8 5 4
                 ♠ 10
                 ♡ 10 8 7 6 3 2
                 ◇ K 9 3 2
                 ♣ A J
```

This was the bidding in an Olympiad match between the USA and Sweden:

South	West	North	East
Hamman	Sundelin	Wolff	Flodquist
—	—	—	2◇[1]
No	2♡[2]	No	2♠
3♡[3]	4♠	5♡	dble
No	No	No	

[1] The multicoloured two diamonds, usually a weak two bid in hearts or spades.
[2] The standard response, since if his partner's suit is hearts (as seems likely) he wants to go no higher.
[3] Bold, but in a way safer than coming in on the first round. If South had passed at this point his side might have been shut out of the auction.

South ruffed the spade lead and exited with a heart, won by West. Sundelin tried a low club, which ran to the jack. Hamman cashed the ace of clubs, then led a second heart. East played a diamond and South might have succeeded now by winning with the king of diamonds and playing off all his trumps, squeezing West. Instead, he let the ◇ 8 run to dummy and lost a diamond trick later.

The critics pointed out that South is better placed if he cashes one or two diamonds before exiting in trumps. That is so, but Hamman no doubt counted East for six spades rather than seven. Then if East held three diamonds he might make a diamond trick.

The best play, perhaps, is to cash the king of diamonds before exiting with the second heart. This will ensure the contract unless East began with Q J x of diamonds as well as six spades to the ace and the ace of hearts. I very much doubt whether the armchair critics worked out all the complexities of the play.

30

Change of luck in transfer market

When teams or pairs from the same country reach the final of a big event, they are usually matched against one another in an early round. If you ask why, you will be told: 'We don't want you to meet near the finish when one of you might be out of the running and might be suspected of giving a push to your friends.' Such innocence! Players from the same country play with intense rivalry against one another, whatever the circumstances. I can imagine the emotions caused by this deal from the Swiss event at Seattle, when two Australian teams were in opposition.

Dealer East	♠ 8 5 4
Game all	♡ —
	◇ A K J 9 7
	♣ Q J 10 6 4

♠ K J 10 7 6	♠ 9 2
♡ 10	♡ A Q 7 5 4 3 2
◇ Q 6 5 4	◇ 3 2
♣ 8 7 3	♣ K 9

♠ A Q 3
♡ K J 9 8 6
◇ 10 8
♣ A 5 2

This was the bidding at the first table:

South	West	North	East
—	—	—	No
1NT	No	2♣	2♡
dble	No	No	No

A well-judged pass by North, as it turned out, and an enjoyable 1100 for South – John Lester, who at one time was a well-known player in Britain.

But you never know. This was the auction at the other table, where four of Australia's leading players were engaged:

South	West	North	East
Gill	Burgess	Klinger	Marston
—	—	—	3♡
No	No	4NT[1]	No
6♣[2]	dble	No	No
No			

[1] An overbid on the values held, but it is difficult to express the hand accurately.
[2] I like it!

South ruffed the heart lead in dummy, ran the queen of clubs, and followed with the 10 of clubs, which was covered by the king and ace. At this point South can count eleven tricks if the diamonds go well, and the twelfth may come from a spade ruff. Gill ran the 10 of diamonds, cashed the ace of spades, then played three more rounds of diamonds, discarding two spades from hand. Now he ruffed a spade and lost just one trick at the finish, for a score of 1540 and a gain of 10 IMPs.

This deal from a match between Taiwan and New Zealand in the Far Eastern Championship was similar in many ways:

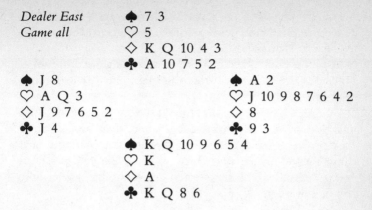

Dealer East   ♠ 7 3
Game all   ♡ 5
              ◇ K Q 10 4 3
              ♣ A 10 7 5 2

♠ J 8   ♠ A 2
♡ A Q 3   ♡ J 10 9 8 7 6 4 2
◇ J 9 7 6 5 2   ◇ 8
♣ J 4   ♣ 9 3

              ♠ K Q 10 9 6 5 4
              ♡ K
              ◇ A
              ♣ K Q 8 6

The Taiwan East opened three hearts. What do you think South should do? A jump to four spades is the cautious, not to say the sensible, action, but Mayer, for New Zealand, launched himself into 4NT. His partner, Cornell, appeared to think this was the unusual notrump, indicating a minor two-suiter. He responded 5NT, forcing his partner to six spades, which had to go one down after the lead of the ace of hearts.

It looks a poor result for North–South, but as I remarked before, you never know. This was the bidding at the other table:

South	West	North	East
Huang	Sims	Chen	Marston
—	—	—	3♡
4♠	No	5♣	No
5◇	No	5♡	No
5NT	No	6◇	No
7♠	No	No	dble
7NT	dble	No	No
No			

103

I don't know enough about the players' methods to criticize this auction with any authority, but it does seem to me that North did too much.

Just 2600 points later, New Zealand had gained 21 IMPs. Note that the slam bid at the other table made a difference of only 1 point.

You may have noted that the Australian East on the first deal was named Marston, and so was the New Zealand East on the second deal. Yes, it was Paul Marston each time. He and his partner, Burgess, after many successes in New Zealand were transferred to Australia; rather like football players.

31

When is a blind spot not a blind spot?

Earlier in this book I wrote about 'blind spots', implying that more often than not such plays were simple errors. Naturally, it wasn't long before I had a most expensive blind spot myself in a Gold Cup match. With four tricks to cash in a suit, I played them off (as I thought), then conceded the remainder, claiming my contract of 3NT. Unfortunately, one of the winners was still nestling among my remaining cards. The opponents, quite fairly, claimed one down. The opposition at the other table were not in game and my error made a difference of 16 IMPs.

When a small disaster like this has occurred, Irving Rose becomes a dangerous partner. In the second half of the match we held these cards as North–South:

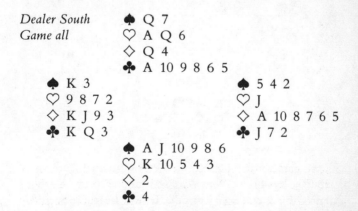

Dealer South
Game all

♠ Q 7
♡ A Q 6
◇ Q 4
♣ A 10 9 8 6 5

♠ K 3   ♠ 5 4 2
♡ 9 8 7 2   ♡ J
◇ K J 9 3 ◇ A 10 8 7 6 5
♣ K Q 3   ♣ J 7 2

♠ A J 10 9 8 6
♡ K 10 5 4 3
◇ 2
♣ 4

This time Rose was South. He opened the bidding – I don't mind that – and later pushed on with an imprudent

4NT. Six spades might have been on – but it wasn't.

When the pairs met at the end of the match I said to our team-mates, Dixon and Sheehan, 'I suppose they didn't get to a slam on board so-and-so?'

'No, they played in four hearts.'

'We've lost, then,' said Rose.

When we came to this hand, Sheehan explained the play at his table. Diamond lead and return, foolishly ruffed; A Q of hearts, then the spade queen, ducked, and another spade, which lost to the king. Now Sheehan played another diamond. South ruffed in hand and led a spade, ruffed by West. Another diamond – and South finished two down; 3 IMPs to the good guys, and we won the match by 2!

Finally, a deal played between Britain and Italy in the European Championship a few years ago:

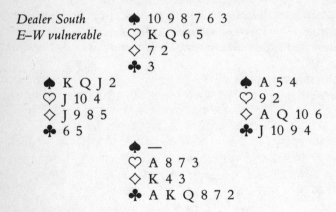

Dealer South
E–W vulnerable

♠ 10 9 8 7 6 3
♡ K Q 6 5
♢ 7 2
♣ 3

♠ K Q J 2
♡ J 10 4
♢ J 9 8 5
♣ 6 5

♠ A 5 4
♡ 9 2
♢ A Q 10 6
♣ J 10 9 4

♠ —
♡ A 8 7 3
♢ K 4 3
♣ A K Q 8 7 2

The Italian South opened one heart – normal in most of the Italian systems. West passed and North, perhaps influenced by the score, jumped to four hearts. South bid six hearts, a reasonable venture.

South ruffed the spade lead, played the ace of clubs and ruffed a club, then led a diamond from dummy. East went in with the ace and continued with the spade attack. Now South drew trumps, came to hand with the king of diamonds, and claimed twelve tricks by way of five clubs, four trumps in dummy, two ruffs and the king of diamonds.

Go back for a moment to the point at which East was in with the ace of diamonds:

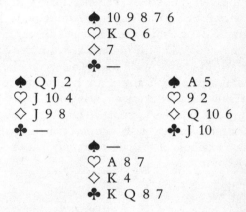

Now the spade from East looked natural but was the *only* play to give South the contract. He needs a ruff for his twelfth trick and on any other return there is an entry problem.

'Sorry,' said East, when he realized what he had done. 'It was a blind spot.' Poor fellow! He never heard the end of it.

32

Champions pounce on every mistake

I had the very pleasant experience one year of going to Hong Kong to do the Vugraph commentary on the Far Eastern Championships. In particular, I was interested to study the methods of the Indonesian team that had done so well in world events. Well, there's no secret: they play well and ruthlessly punish any error by the opposition. The final result on this occasion was Indonesia 118 victory points, Taiwan 104, Australia 102.

This deal from Indonesia's critical match against Taiwan is a good example of the concentration that the champions bring to bear.

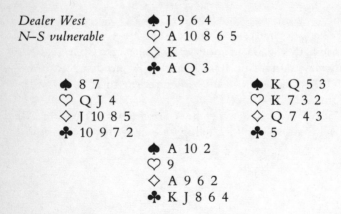

Dealer West
N–S vulnerable

```
                    ♠ J 9 6 4
                    ♡ A 10 8 6 5
                    ◇ K
                    ♣ A Q 3
    ♠ 8 7                         ♠ K Q 5 3
    ♡ Q J 4                       ♡ K 7 3 2
    ◇ J 10 8 5                    ◇ Q 7 4 3
    ♣ 10 9 7 2                    ♣ 5
                    ♠ A 10 2
                    ♡ 9
                    ◇ A 9 6 2
                    ♣ K J 8 6 4
```

In the closed room Sakul and Waluyan bid and made the cast-iron 3NT on the North–South cards. The Taiwan sequence led to a less orthodox contract:

South	West	North	East
Kuo	Manoppo	Hau	Lasut
—	No	2♡	No
2NT	No	3♣	No
4♣	No	No	No

North's two hearts presumably carried the same message as the Flannery two diamonds in America – a limited hand with 4–5 in the majors. I have always thought this an uneconomical use for a conventional bid. What is wrong with one heart on the North hand?

West led a club, won in dummy. The declarer played a spade to the 10 and was happy to see it win the trick. He cashed the ace of spades and turned to the clubs. Lasut cleverly allowed the queen to hold, pounced on the third round, and drew South's last trump. This left Kuo with no way to unravel his entries.

The best play on the declarer's hand, after the 10 of spades has won, is certainly not obvious. As the cards lie, a club continuation works well.

This next hand, from the match between Indonesia and Australia, presented the Indonesian East with a most unusual problem.

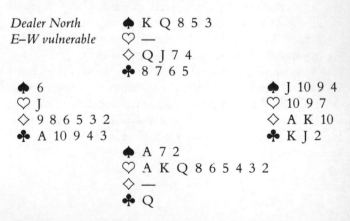

Dealer North
E–W vulnerable

North
♠ K Q 8 5 3
♡ —
♢ Q J 7 4
♣ 8 7 6 5

West
♠ 6
♡ J
♢ 9 8 6 5 3 2
♣ A 10 9 4 3

East
♠ J 10 9 4
♡ 10 9 7
♢ A K 10
♣ K J 2

South
♠ A 7 2
♡ A K Q 8 6 5 4 3 2
♢ —
♣ Q

109

The North–South pair for Australia was Burgess and Marston. This pair, originally from New Zealand, play a variation of the strong pass system. They play it well and have achieved many successes at international level. Partly, of course, this is due not so much to the superiority of their methods as to the unfamiliar problems they present. You may sit with a long account of the system at your elbow, but when a comparatively rare sequence occurs you cannot be sure how your partner will regard any action you propose to take.

On this occasion Marston, North, opened one diamond, indicating 8–12 points and at least four spades. After eight rounds of scientific exploration Burgess, having discovered that his partner held ♠ K Q x x x, no hearts, and a minimum hand with no ace, settled in the unbeatable contract of six hearts. A triumph for the system, but . . .

West led the 6 of spades. (His partner was marked with an ace and it might have been the ace of spades.) Burgess won in hand, drew trumps, and led a spade to dummy. This in itself was odd, because there might have been a squeeze for seven – if East had held four spades and A K of clubs, for example.

When West discarded on the second spade, Burgess, possibly exhausted by the rigours of the tortuous auction, *ducked*. Hikmat (East) knew that Burgess had had a brainstorm because he had a complete count of the hand. He still had to guess which minor ace to cash.

It was like being offered £1000 to nothing on the toss of a coin. There was a small indication, however: with ♣ A Q 10 9 x x West might have overcalled on the first round. To the cheers of his compatriots (and most of the audience) Hikmat switched to a club to scupper the 'unbeatable' slam.

33

Leading lights

Semper aliquid novum ex Africa, as (I think) Tacitus remarked. Alec Traub, of Cape Town, sent me a fascinating deal. First, there is a lead problem. At game all you hold in the West position:

♠ K
♡ A 9 6 3 2
♢ 3
♣ Q J 10 8 7 3

South, on your right, opens five spades and all pass. What do you lead?

The five-spade opening traditionally indicates a hand on which the opener is concerned only with the top honours in the trump suit. On the present occasion South is presumably missing ace and king of spades, and he expects his side suit, diamonds, to be solid. From your side, you must hope that there is a gap in the diamonds.

The disadvantage of leading a club is that dummy may hold the top honours and provide the declarer with discards. If you try the ace of hearts it will surely be ruffed and you may have an awkward lead when you come in with the king of spades.

Of course, you have made up your mind now. You lead the king of spades and the full hand turns out to be:

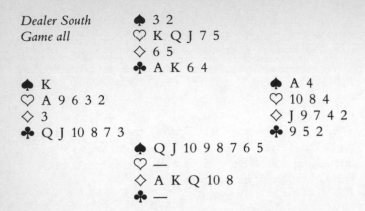

Dealer South
Game all

♠ 3 2
♡ K Q J 7 5
◇ 6 5
♣ A K 6 4

♠ K
♡ A 9 6 3 2
◇ 3
♣ Q J 10 8 7 3

♠ A 4
♡ 10 8 4
◇ J 9 7 4 2
♣ 9 5 2

♠ Q J 10 9 8 7 6 5
♡ —
◇ A K Q 10 8
♣ —

But is the king of spades, followed by the ace of hearts, good enough? No, South will ruff and play off the ace and king of diamonds; then he will ruff a diamond and take a discard on the ace of clubs.

But East is there and, we trust, alert. Realizing that the only chance for the defence is to win diamond tricks, he overtakes the king of spades with the ace and plays a second round. South may play ◇ A K and exit with a low diamond, but now East can lead a heart and the defence will make another trick.

This deal has a somewhat artificial air, I agree. The next one occurred at rubber bridge and I can vouch for its authenticity. To begin with, suppose, as South, you hold:

♠ K Q 10 9 7 4
♡ —
◇ A J 10 7 5
♣ A 4

Your partner, who is vulnerable, opens one diamond; East, who is not, overcalls with three hearts.

Now it certainly looks as though partner should hold the ace of spades, so a grand slam is likely. Most players would begin with something like four hearts, the enemy suit, but whether this would help very much is doubtful. At any rate, the present South stood not upon the order of his going (whatever that silly phrase means) but went straight to seven diamonds, presumably to make it difficult for the opponents to judge whether or not to sacrifice. This was the full deal:

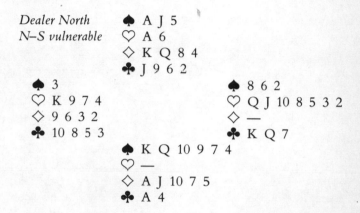

Dealer North
N–S vulnerable

North
♠ A J 5
♡ A 6
♢ K Q 8 4
♣ J 9 6 2

West
♠ 3
♡ K 9 7 4
♢ 9 6 3 2
♣ 10 8 5 3

East
♠ 8 6 2
♡ Q J 10 8 5 3 2
♢ —
♣ K Q 7

South
♠ K Q 10 9 7 4
♡ —
♢ A J 10 7 5
♣ A 4

South's seven diamonds was not the end of the story. The bidding continued:

South	West	North	East
—	—	1♢	3♡
7♢	7♡	No	No
7♠	dble	No	No
No			

West led a diamond and his partner ruffed. Now West was not a tournament player, but when asked why he doubled seven spades he answered as follows:

'When North passed seven hearts on the round before, I assumed that he held the ace of hearts and was giving his partner a chance to bid 7NT. When South bid seven spades

113

instead, it was obvious that he held length in spades as well as diamonds. If I let seven spades run to East, and he was void of diamonds, he might double for a diamond lead, and then North might run to 7NT. So I thought I would double first and not make it so easy for North.'

34

Tricky solution lost in fog

Like many writers on the game, I dare say, I often notice an interesting deal, either at the table or elsewhere, scribble it down and some time later cannot remember what it was all about. This one was a real puzzle:

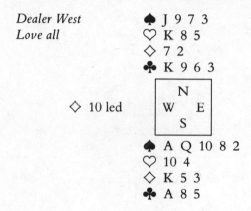

Dealer West
Love all

♠ J 9 7 3
♡ K 8 5
♢ 7 2
♣ K 9 6 3

◇ 10 led

♠ A Q 10 8 2
♡ 10 4
♢ K 5 3
♣ A 8 5

4 ♠, after West has opened one heart, my note implied. The bidding might have been:

South	West	North	East
—	1♡	No	2◇
2♠	No	4♣	No
No	No		

North's four spades is on the forward side, but he is entitled to think that his kings will be well placed.

Diamond to ace, heart to West's ace, heart queen to

dummy's king. But what then? South has lost two tricks, the spade finesse must be wrong, and there is a sure loser in clubs.

I looked at this for a long while before light began to dawn. Suppose the full deal were something like this:

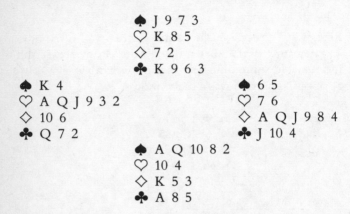

Diamond to ace, heart to ace, heart to dummy's king. Suppose now that you ruff the third heart, cash the king of diamonds, then exit with ace and another spade. Do you see what might happen? West might place you with 5–2–2–4 distribution. If so, he will lead a *heart*, giving you (as he thinks) a useless ruff-and-discard.

Perhaps you looked for another solution? Cash ace and king of clubs, play ace of spades, then eliminate the red suits and give West the lead with the king of spades. This plan won't work, because East is marked with six diamonds and it is impossible for West to hold only four cards in the black suits.

Another hand that puzzled me when I looked at it after an interval was the following:

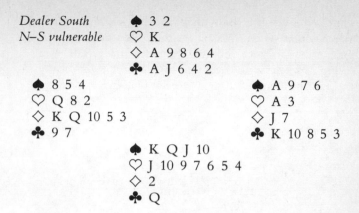

Dealer South
N–S vulnerable

	♠ 3 2	
	♡ K	
	◇ A 9 8 6 4	
	♣ A J 6 4 2	

♠ 8 5 4		♠ A 9 7 6
♡ Q 8 2		♡ A 3
◇ K Q 10 5 3		◇ J 7
♣ 9 7		♣ K 10 8 5 3

	♠ K Q J 10	
	♡ J 10 9 7 6 5 4	
	◇ 2	
	♣ Q	

I had a note that the deal had been defended by a Canadian player. This was the bidding:

South	West	North	East
—	—	No	1♠[1]
2♡	2♠	dble[2]	No
3♡	No	4♡[3]	No
No	No		

[1] He may have been playing a one-club system, but I think it more likely that he opened the high-valued suit in the hope of winning the part-score battle.

[2] A competitive double, indicating values in the two unbid suits.

[3] Sporting, with a partner who passed originally.

Spade lead, one down, said my note. Why one down? It looks as though the defence will take just a spade and two hearts.

Try again. West, having supported spades, leads his top card, the 8, and East holds off. South plays a heart to the king and ace. Now East plays another *low* spade, and the effect is that when West takes the queen of hearts he can put partner in with the ace of spades and ruff the fourth round. Somehow, it is easy to miss.

35

Watching heads fall into the basket

There is nothing the spectators like better than seeing a reputedly good player make a muddle of an easy hand. 'I couldn't quite understand . . .' they say, hoping for more details before they recount the story. It took South a long time to live down the following episode.

Dealer West
Love all

	♠ —
	♡ 7 6 4 3
	◇ J 10 9 4 3
	♣ A 8 7 6

♠ A Q J 9 8		♠ K 7 6 5 2
♡ J 9		♡ Q 8
◇ K 7		◇ 2
♣ K J 10 9		♣ Q 5 4 3 2

	♠ 10 4 3
	♡ A K 10 5 2
	◇ A Q 8 6 5
	♣ —

South	West	North	East
—	1♠	No	3♠
4♡	4♠	5♡	No
No	5♠	6♡	No
No	dble	No	No
No			

In tournament play South might have presented a better picture of his hand by bidding 3NT over three spades and a number of diamonds on the next round. However, this type of manoeuvre can go wrong at rubber bridge.

West led the ace of spades against six hearts doubled and South was pleased by the sight of dummy. There seemed to be two chances for the contract: the diamond finesse, or playing the heart suit for no loser. The natural line is a trump to the ace, cash the king, ruff another spade, and discard the last spade on the ace of clubs. Then, as the cards lie, you will be taking a diamond finesse for the overtrick.

If this had been the sequence of play the *tricoteuses* beside the guillotine would not have looked up from their knitting. But South was a player who paid excessive attention to his opponents' bidding. To justify his enterprise, West must be 6–1–1–5, or something like that, he thought. It might be a good plan to take the diamond finesse first and deal with the hearts later.

Perhaps it was well reasoned – I'm not sure. All I can say is that North was not appreciative when West won the diamond lead and gave his partner a ruff. And the kibitzers had a field-day.

Shortly after that little episode I held the South cards on this deal from match play:

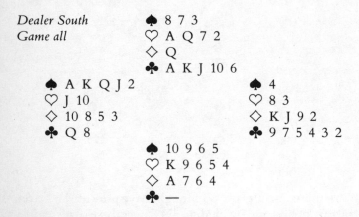

Dealer South
Game all

	♠ 8 7 3	
	♡ A Q 7 2	
	◇ Q	
	♣ A K J 10 6	
♠ A K Q J 2		♠ 4
♡ J 10		♡ 8 3
◇ 10 8 5 3		◇ K J 9 2
♣ Q 8		♣ 9 7 5 4 3 2
	♠ 10 9 6 5	
	♡ K 9 6 5 4	
	◇ A 7 6 4	
	♣ —	

South	West	North	East
No	1♠	dble	No
3♡	No	4♡	No
No	No		

West began with three rounds of spades. At my table East discarded the 3 of clubs on the second round and a 'helpful' 9 of diamonds on the third. West obediently switched to the 3 of diamonds and I wrapped up 10 tricks easily enough.

It seemed a flat board, but I noticed that my partner was looking closely at the opposing cards. Then I realized what was interesting him.

At the other table, we learned later, South had opened with two hearts, meaning heaven knows what. The final contract was the same, but on the third round of spades East had discarded the 2 of diamonds. This was sensible, because if West had held the ace he would naturally have cashed it. Instead, West continued with a fourth spade, which South was obliged to ruff with dummy's queen of hearts.

When the 10 of hearts fell under the ace, South had a small problem. Reflecting that with ♡ J 10 West might have dropped the jack, he finessed on the next round and lost the contract. His play, it must be admitted, was in line with the principle of restricted choice, the theory being that with J 10 West might have dropped the other card, while with a singleton 10 he would have had no alternative.

36

Special pleasure in declarer's undoing

Some of the prettiest defences involve a successful assault on declarer's (or dummy's) entries. One moment he seems to have all the tricks he needs, and the next they slip tantalizingly out of his grasp.

```
Dealer North        ♠ Q 4
Game all            ♡ K 5
                    ♢ K Q J 7 6 3
                    ♣ A K 4
  ♠ A K J 6 2                        ♠ 10 8 3
  ♡ 10 9 8 2                         ♡ 4
  ♢ A 8                              ♢ 10 5 2
  ♣ J 9                              ♣ Q 10 6 5 3 2
                    ♠ 9 7 5
                    ♡ A Q J 7 6 3
                    ♢ 9 4
                    ♣ 8 7
```

South	West	North	East
—	—	1♢	No
1♡	1♠	2♣	No
2♡	No	2♠	No
3♡	No	4♡	No
No	No		

North was intending to rebid 2NT over his partner's one heart, and the spade intervention was awkward. He might have bid three diamonds, but his choice of two clubs was sensible enough.

South may seem to have only three losers in a heart contract, but the defence can create problems. West in fact began with three rounds of spades, forcing dummy to ruff. Declarer led the king of hearts, but did not overtake as he had an idea what was happening. The position was now:

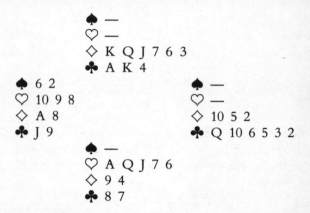

♠ —
♡ —
◇ K Q J 7 6 3
♣ A K 4

♠ 6 2
♡ 10 9 8
◇ A 8
♣ J 9

♠ —
♡ —
◇ 10 5 2
♣ Q 10 6 5 3 2

♠ —
♡ A Q J 7 6
◇ 9 4
♣ 8 7

West captured the king of diamonds with the ace and exited with a diamond. Now South could not leave the dummy without establishing a trump trick for West.

'Well played, partner,' said East at the end of the hand. 'But shouldn't you have held up the ace of diamonds for a round? South might have held 10 x and you'd have given him an entry.'

'I thought about that,' West replied. 'But if I do hold up the ace, declarer may cash the ace and king of clubs before exiting from dummy with a second diamond. Then I can't do him any damage.'

Study this next deal: do you think that South should make four hearts or not?

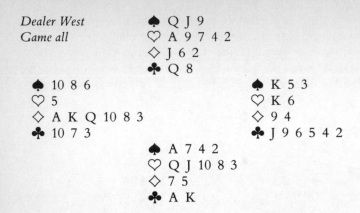

Dealer West   ♠ Q J 9
Game all   ♡ A 9 7 4 2
                     ◇ J 6 2
                     ♣ Q 8

♠ 10 8 6   ♠ K 5 3
♡ 5   ♡ K 6
◇ A K Q 10 8 3   ◇ 9 4
♣ 10 7 3   ♣ J 9 6 5 4 2

                     ♠ A 7 4 2
                     ♡ Q J 10 8 3
                     ◇ 7 5
                     ♣ A K

Some players won't open with a pre-empt when their
suit is more or less solid, but West suffered from no such
inhibitions. He opened three diamonds and the bidding
continued:

South	West	North	East
—	3◇	No	No
3♡	No	4♡	No
No	No		

The defence began with three rounds of diamonds,
South ruffing the third round. Declarer led the queen of
hearts and played the ace from dummy, both because the
finesse was sure to be wrong and because he had visions of
an end-play. He cashed two top clubs and exited with a
trump. Now East was forced to open up the spades or
concede a ruff-and-discard, so the declarer lost no spade
trick and made his contract.

It is apparent that if South finesses the heart, allowing
East a safe exit, he must lose a spade eventually. (The right
defence, of course, is to cover the second spade honour,
not the first.)

East accorded South a nod of congratulation and no

124

more was said. But in the middle of the next rubber it struck East that an unusual play would have beaten the contract. If East ruffs the third diamond with the king of hearts and exits with a trump or a club, he makes his spade in due course.

37

Dazzling play, but the game is over

'Is it true, as you imply,' a correspondent enquired, 'that many bridge brilliancies are conceived in the post-mortem?' Few diamonds are both flawless and top colour, I agree, but even if the best play was not made at the table it may still be instructive for a future occasion.

Here is a hand that Robert Sheehan played during the World Olympiad in Seattle:

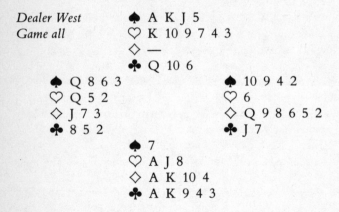

Dealer West
Game all

```
                    ♠ A K J 5
                    ♡ K 10 9 7 4 3
                    ◇ —
                    ♣ Q 10 6
  ♠ Q 8 6 3                          ♠ 10 9 4 2
  ♡ Q 5 2                            ♡ 6
  ◇ J 7 3                            ◇ Q 9 8 6 5 2
  ♣ 8 5 2                            ♣ J 7
                    ♠ 7
                    ♡ A J 8
                    ◇ A K 10 4
                    ♣ A K 9 4 3
```

North–South had to compete against one of those pairs whose system included an opening bid on 'nothing'. Whether West's opening one diamond on this occasion signified 0–10 points or some subdivision, I cannot say. At any rate, North–South had agreed to ignore the opening bid, so that North's one heart in the following sequence was equal to a normal one-heart opening.

South	West	North	East
Sheehan		Rose	
—	1◇	1♡	No
2♣	No	2♠	No
3♡	No	4♣	No
4NT	No	5◇	No
5NT[1]	No	6♡[2]	No
7NT[3]	No	No	No

[1] 4NT for aces, followed by 5NT for kings, the old Blackwood arrangement, has gone out of fashion. Here 5NT asked simply about partner's holding in the long suit, hearts.

[2] Showing a six-card suit with one of the top honours.

[3] He cannot exactly count thirteen tricks, but even if the hearts don't break there should be other chances. In tournament play grand slams do not require such good odds as at rubber bridge.

West led a low diamond – a poor choice because it left him with a card to keep in diamonds as well as in the major suits. The contract can be made in a number of ways, obviously, but South went one down at the table.

'If only my play had matched the bidding,' Sheehan lamented. 'Obviously if the heart queen drops in two rounds there are 13 top tricks. But watch what happens if I resist the temptation to find out my fate at once. I discard a club from dummy at trick one, and after winning with the ◇ A I follow with five rounds of clubs, discarding two hearts and a spade from dummy. This is the 7-card ending:

♠ A K J
♡ K 10 9 7
◇ —
♣ —

♠ Q 8   ♠ 10 9 4
♡ Q 5 2   ♡ 6
◇ J 7   ◇ 9 8 6
♣ —   ♣ —

♠ 7
♡ A J 8
◇ K 10 4
♣ —

'When I cash the spades West is squeezed. Even if he were not, I have obtained enough vital clues to tell me how to play the critical suit, hearts.'

Some players will describe a difficult play so convincingly that for a time you won't realize that a simpler line would also have worked. This was a typical Martin Hoffman story:

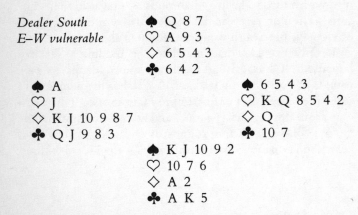

Dealer South
E–W vulnerable

♠ Q 8 7
♡ A 9 3
◇ 6 5 4 3
♣ 6 4 2

♠ A   ♠ 6 5 4 3
♡ J   ♡ K Q 8 5 4 2
◇ K J 10 9 8 7   ◇ Q
♣ Q J 9 8 3   ♣ 10 7

♠ K J 10 9 2
♡ 10 7 6
◇ A 2
♣ A K 5

South played in three spades after West had shown his minor two-suiter. East overtook the heart lead and

128

returned his singleton diamond, won by the ace. West won the next trick with the ace of spades and cashed the king of diamonds.

The defenders have five tricks on top and if they play accurately they can prevent South from developing a squeeze. However, East discarded a club on the second diamond and another club on the third round. South ruffed and this was the position:

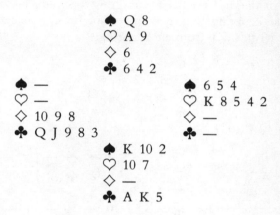

♠ Q 8
♡ A 9
◇ 6
♣ 6 4 2

♠ —   ♠ 6 5 4
♡ —   ♡ K 8 5 4 2
◇ 10 9 8 ◇ —
♣ Q J 9 8 3 ♣ —

♠ K 10 2
♡ 10 7
◇ —
♣ A K 5

'Do you see what happens now?' asked Martin. 'The declarer plays the 10 of spades to the queen, overtakes the 8 with the king, and exits with the 2. East has to return a heart and West is squeezed.'

Yes, very pretty; but it struck me later that a simpler line is to draw trumps in the usual way, then lead a heart to the 9. East must return a heart and West is squeezed.

38

Times when you can count on success

When players speak of 'counting the hands' they usually think of the declarer performing this task; which is odd, because counting is just as important for the defenders. Consider this deal from rubber bridge:

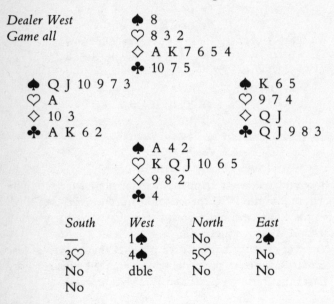

Dealer West
Game all

	♠ 8	
	♡ 8 3 2	
	◇ A K 7 6 5 4	
	♣ 10 7 5	
♠ Q J 10 9 7 3		♠ K 6 5
♡ A		♡ 9 7 4
◇ 10 3		◇ Q J
♣ A K 6 2		♣ Q J 9 8 3
	♠ A 4 2	
	♡ K Q J 10 6 5	
	◇ 9 8 2	
	♣ 4	

South	West	North	East
—	1♠	No	2♠
3♡	4♠	5♡	No
No	dble	No	No
No			

West led the king of clubs, East signalled with the queen, and West followed with another club, which South ruffed. The declarer cashed ace of spades and ruffed a spade, returned with a club ruff, and ruffed his third spade. When a round of trumps followed, West found himself on lead in this six-card ending:

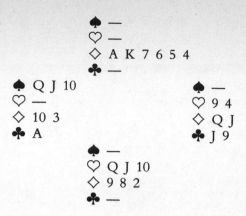

♠ —
♡ —
◇ A K 7 6 5 4
♣ —

♠ Q J 10   ♠ —
♡ —   ♡ 9 4
◇ 10 3   ◇ Q J
♣ A   ♣ J 9

♠ —
♡ Q J 10
◇ 9 8 2
♣ —

With the superficial idea of shortening declarer's trumps,
West continued with the queen of spades. South ruffed,
drew the outstanding trumps, and made the last three
tricks in diamonds.

What strikes you about this sequence of play? First, it
should have been very easy for West to count the declarer's
hand: nothing could be done if South was 7–2 in the red
suits, but if he was 6–3 a diamond switch after the ace of
hearts would leave him stranded in dummy. Second, the
declarer's own play was not bright: he should have cashed
the top diamonds before playing a round of trumps.

The defence on the next hand was more difficult:

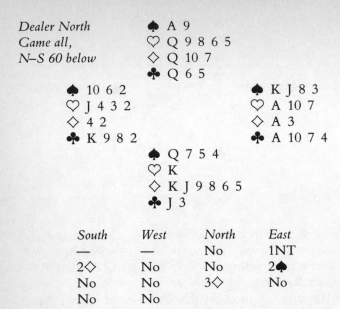

Dealer North
Game all,
N–S 60 below

♠ A 9
♡ Q 9 8 6 5
♢ Q 10 7
♣ Q 6 5

♠ 10 6 2
♡ J 4 3 2
♢ 4 2
♣ K 9 8 2

♠ K J 8 3
♡ A 10 7
♢ A 3
♣ A 10 7 4

♠ Q 7 5 4
♡ K
♢ K J 9 8 6 5
♣ J 3

South	West	North	East
—	—	No	1NT
2♢	No	No	2♠
No	No	3♢	No
No	No		

A spade lead would have provided five easy tricks for the defence, but West chose to lead a club. When dummy played low, East thought about inserting the 10. Finally he decided to play the ace and return a club. West could see that the queen of clubs would provide a discard, so he led a heart to his partner's ace. The position was now:

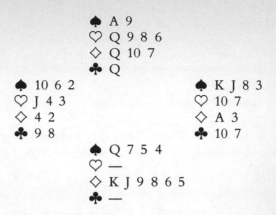

♠ A 9
♡ Q 9 8 6
◇ Q 10 7
♣ Q

♠ 10 6 2   ♠ K J 8 3
♡ J 4 3   ♡ 10 7
◇ 4 2   ◇ A 3
♣ 9 8   ♣ 10 7

♠ Q 7 5 4
♡ —
◇ K J 9 8 6 5
♣ —

At this point East played the ace and another diamond, hoping to make his king of spades eventually. But South played the queen of hearts and ruffed a heart, returned to dummy with a trump, and ruffed another heart; then a spade to the ace, and the remaining spades went away on the fifth heart and the queen of clubs.

'If only you'd led a spade,' East lamented.

'I think we're all right if you cash the ace of hearts at trick two,' West replied. 'Then you lead a club to the king and I return a spade while you still have the ace of diamonds.'

I don't say this was an easy defence to find, but if East thinks along the right lines he can hardly miss it. He can be fairly sure that South has at least four spades, since West did not support; he is marked with two clubs; he must have at least one heart, and probably six diamonds. Thus East can see the way to five defensive tricks so long as he cashes the ace of hearts at trick two. He will follow with a club, and then West will lead a spade.

39

Invigorated by mountain air

This deal from the annual tournament at Crans-sur-Sierre provided both sides with opportunities for expert play.

Dealer East
N–S vulnerable

	♠ J 3 2	
	♡ A J 9 5	
	◇ A 7 6 4 3	
	♣ 2	

♠ 8 4		♠ K Q 10 9 6 5
♡ K 7		♡ 6 2
◇ Q 9 8 5		◇ K J
♣ A K 10 9 5		♣ Q 4 3

	♠ A 7	
	♡ Q 10 8 4 3	
	◇ 10 2	
	♣ J 8 7 6	

South	West	North	East
—	—	—	2♠
No	No	dble[1]	No
4♡[2]	No	No	No

[1] Borderline, obviously, but tournament players, especially in a pairs event, hate to be silenced by a preemptive opening. North's hand has one slight merit: if partner responds three clubs, he can bid three diamonds, offering a choice between the red suits. If North had been 3–4–1–5, with the same values, the double would have been too dangerous.

[2] Also marginal; partner might, of course, have been stronger.

West led the ace of clubs, then switched to the 8 of spades. You have the advantage of seeing all four hands. How would you have played this contract?

As both you and your partner have overbid – or, at least, bid optimistically – you have to make some favourable assumptions. You won't have much chance unless West began with K x of hearts. Even then, you can count only nine tricks – seven in the trump suit and two aces. But perhaps something can be done with dummy's diamonds. It is not easy to see at first, but it is good play to duck the first spade. You will see why in a moment.

East led a second spade and South won. Then he crossed to the ace of diamonds and led dummy's third spade, discarding the second diamond from his own hand and so averting an overruff. Now the defence had no more ammunition. East returned a trump, which was as good as anything, but South, with the aid of the trump finesse, had enough entries to set up a long diamond.

What about the defence? An attack on dummy's entries at trick two would have made South's task more difficult.

My second example of expert play occurred at rubber bridge.

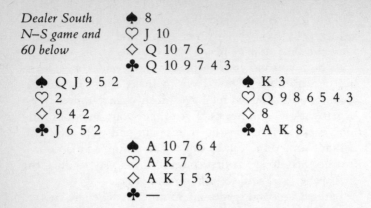

Dealer South
N–S game and
60 below

♠ 8
♡ J 10
♢ Q 10 7 6
♣ Q 10 9 7 4 3

♠ Q J 9 5 2
♡ 2
♢ 9 4 2
♣ J 6 5 2

♠ K 3
♡ Q 9 8 6 5 4 3
♢ 8
♣ A K 8

♠ A 10 7 6 4
♡ A K 7
♢ A K J 5 3
♣ —

I held the West cards, Zia Mahmood was South, and both sides had several hundred points above the line when Zia dealt this hand at 60 up. The bidding went:

South	West	North	East
1♠	No	1NT	2♡
6♢	No	No	No

There are some stolid alternatives to six diamonds, but they would not appeal to Zia. He won the heart lead, cashed the ace of spades and ruffed a spade, noting the fall of East's king. He came back to hand with a trump, ruffed a spade with the ♢ 10, and played a club from dummy. After another spade ruff and a second club ruff he arrived at this position:

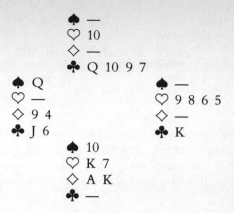

```
              ♠ —
              ♡ 10
              ◇ —
              ♣ Q 10 9 7
♠ Q                          ♠ —
♡ —                          ♡ 9 8 6 5
◇ 9 4                        ◇ —
♣ J 6                        ♣ K
              ♠ 10
              ♡ K 7
              ◇ A K
              ♣ —
```

Zia drew my trumps, parting with two of dummy's clubs. Then he crossed to the ♡ 10 and played a club, using East's ♣ K as a stepping-stone to enjoy his remaining heart.

'Lucky to find four diamonds in dummy,' a kibitzer remarked. 'Still, I must say he played it well.' I cannot improve on that.

40

Power of positive thinking

Hercule Poirot never disguised his contempt for detectives who scurried hither and thither in pursuit of clues instead of sitting back and using their 'little grey cells'. The declarer on this first hand was presented with the evidence he needed.

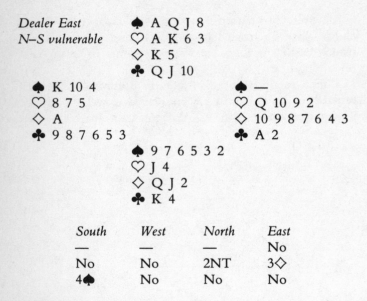

Dealer East
N–S vulnerable

♠ A Q J 8
♡ A K 6 3
◇ K 5
♣ Q J 10

♠ K 10 4
♡ 8 7 5
◇ A
♣ 9 8 7 6 5 3

♠ —
♡ Q 10 9 2
◇ 10 9 8 7 6 4 3
♣ A 2

♠ 9 7 6 5 3 2
♡ J 4
◇ Q J 2
♣ K 4

South	West	North	East
—	—	—	No
No	No	2NT	3◇
4♠	No	No	No

West led the ace of diamonds, East played the 3, and West was not hard pressed to find the switch to a club. In with the ace of clubs, East returned a diamond and West ruffed. West now exited with a club and South led a spade, on which West produced the 10. After brief consideration the declarer played dummy's jack and so made the contract.

'Thank you, partner,' said North admiringly. 'You took a good view of the spades. There was room for East to hold the singleton king, wasn't there?'

'Just about,' South replied. 'But it struck me that if East had held 1–3–7–2 shape he might have opened three diamonds. With 0–4–7–2 players are less inclined to pre-empt.'

This was true, but most players wouldn't have thought of it. The detective work on the next hand had a touch of Holmes rather than Poirot; that is to say, the declarer had to do some work to unravel the clues.

```
Dealer South        ♠ A 9 8 7
Love all            ♡ 4
                    ♢ A Q 10 9 6
                    ♣ A Q 10
♠ 10                              ♠ Q 2
♡ 2                               ♡ A Q J 10 9 6 5 3
♢ J 8 7 5 4 3                     ♢ 2
♣ 9 8 6 4 3                       ♣ 7 5
                    ♠ K J 6 5 4 3
                    ♡ K 8 7
                    ♢ K
                    ♣ K J 2
```

South	West	North	East
1♠	No	3♢	3♡
3♠	No	4♣	4♡
No	No	4NT	5♡
No	No	6♠	No
No	No		

It may look as though nothing much can go wrong for the declarer in six spades, but the defenders can make the play quite difficult. East won the heart lead and did well to return a heart. South played low and West's 10 of spades forced dummy to overruff with the ace. The declarer led a spade from the table and went up with the king, so losing the contract. 'I had to play the spades that way, knowing the hearts were 8–1,' he remarked.

North didn't argue, but he had an idea that South might have found out more about the distribution. An important clue is that if East had been void in diamonds or clubs he would have doubled six spades. It is safe, therefore, to play a diamond to the king and cross to the queen of clubs to test the effect of the ace of diamonds. Now two possibilities arise:

1. East will discard his second club. Then South discards a club, follows with the queen of diamonds and discards his third club. This is followed by a club from dummy, which will show that East began with one diamond and two clubs; ergo, two spades.

2. East may discard a heart on the ace of diamonds with the idea of concealing his club holding. No matter, South as before discards clubs on the ace and queen of diamonds, then leads a club from dummy. He quickly discovers East's distribution.

41

High drama in duel between old rivals

The final of the world championship in Stockholm between America and Italy was the seventeenth time the two countries had met since the competition for the Bermuda Bowl began in 1951. Italy had won on thirteen occasions, America on four. This time, the Americans began as favourites.

The first 64 boards were fiercely contested. Italy's lead of 9 IMPs owed more to some untypical errors by the Americans than to any great brilliance of their own. This was board 58:

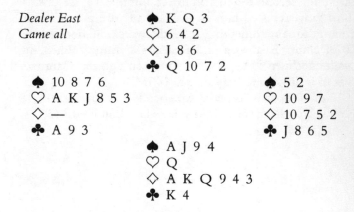

Dealer East
Game all

```
                    ♠ K Q 3
                    ♡ 6 4 2
                    ◇ J 8 6
                    ♣ Q 10 7 2
   ♠ 10 8 7 6                        ♠ 5 2
   ♡ A K J 8 5 3                     ♡ 10 9 7
   ◇ —                               ◇ 10 7 5 2
   ♣ A 9 3                           ♣ J 8 6 5
                    ♠ A J 9 4
                    ♡ Q
                    ◇ A K Q 9 4 3
                    ♣ K 4
```

In the closed room Lauria and Mosca reached the par contract of five diamonds; 600 to Italy.

This was the bidding in the open room:

South	West	North	East
Hamman	Garozzo	Wolff	Belladonna
—	—	—	No
1♣	1♢[1]	dble[2]	No
No	2♡	No	No
2♠[3]	No	4♠[4]	No
No	No		

[1] It appears that the sequence followed by Garozzo signified a fairly strong overcall.

[2] A negative double, of course.

[3] Perhaps this was a mistake? There seems to be no reason why he should not have bid his long suit first.

[4] The double jump, with only three spades, seems misleading.

The defence began with two rounds of hearts. Hamman ruffed the second round and forced out the ace of clubs. A third heart reduced him to just A J of trumps. In a vain attempt to save something from the wreck, he finessed the 10 of clubs. East won and returned a trump. When the spades declined to break . . . but I can't go on! Hamman was four down and Italy gained 14 IMPs.

With 48 boards to play, America led by an anxious 18 points, and this modest lead was reduced on board 150.

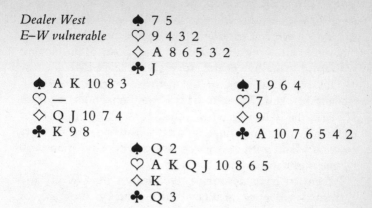

Dealer West
E–W vulnerable

```
                    ♠ 7 5
                    ♡ 9 4 3 2
                    ◇ A 8 6 5 3 2
                    ♣ J
   ♠ A K 10 8 3                    ♠ J 9 6 4
   ♡ —                             ♡ 7
   ◇ Q J 10 7 4                    ◇ 9
   ♣ K 9 8                         ♣ A 10 7 6 5 4 2
                    ♠ Q 2
                    ♡ A K Q J 10 8 6 5
                    ◇ K
                    ♣ Q 3
```

Obviously an explosive deal, on which East–West can make a slam in either black suit. The USA had the better of the argument in the closed room:

South	West	North	East
Becker	Mosca	Rubin	Lauria
—	2♠	No	4♠
5♡	5♠	No	No
6♡	dble	No	No
No			

This cost only 300. It looked like a gain to America, but this was the bidding at the other table:

South	West	North	East
Belladonna	Wolff	Garozzo	Hamman
—	1◇	No	1♠
4♡	4♠	5◇	No
5♡	No	No	No

No doubt Wolff intended his pass of five hearts to be forcing, but Hamman declined to be forced. They never found their club fit and they omitted to double five hearts.

As it turned out, this was just as well. West led the king of spades, on which East played the 4, and West then tried a diamond, allowing Belladonna to dispose of his losing spade and make five hearts, for a swing of 13 IMPs.

This put Italy back in the game, but near the finish Belladonna and Garozzo had a fatal misunderstanding. 4NT, in the Italian system, is sometimes conventional but often has other meanings. On this occasion the partners reached a slam with two aces missing. The Americans won by the minute margin of 5 points.

I seem to have described two deals where Wolff and Hamman had poor results. That's unlucky; they are, of course, a great pair.

The Bermuda Bowl is conducted in a different way nowadays, with teams from several zones contesting the final rounds. We have probably seen the last of the long head-to-head matches.

42

Howlers which inspire a reaction

'Before I watched the bridge experts play on television, I always thought they never made mistakes.'

The speaker was a keen family bridge player. There are others who apparently share her disillusionment. Here are two hands from a world championship match in Stockholm, to put the matter in perspective.

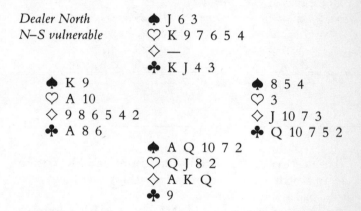

Dealer North
N–S vulnerable

```
                        ♠ J 6 3
                        ♡ K 9 7 6 5 4
                        ◇ —
                        ♣ K J 4 3
    ♠ K 9                              ♠ 8 5 4
    ♡ A 10                             ♡ 3
    ◇ 9 8 6 5 4 2                      ◇ J 10 7 3
    ♣ A 8 6                            ♣ Q 10 7 5 2
                        ♠ A Q 10 7 2
                        ♡ Q J 8 2
                        ◇ A K Q
                        ♣ 9
```

This was board 38 of the semifinal between the American team known as the Aces and another American team, described during this match as the Challengers. A pedestrian four hearts at both tables, you might suppose, and indeed in one room Wold and Passell, for the Challengers, bid four hearts and made five.

To the delight of Wold's supporters, Sontag and Weichsel at the other table, disdaining the use of the 'old Black', reached six hearts, which Meckstroth doubled.

Meckstroth led the ace of hearts 'to have a look at the dummy'. What he saw was not too alarming. South is probably void in clubs, he thought to himself. In any case, the king of spades looked like a trick, and if South had a club loser, where would it go?

He soon found out. South won the heart continuation, discarded two spades from dummy on the ace and king of diamonds, and played ace and 10 of spades, bringing down the king. This left:

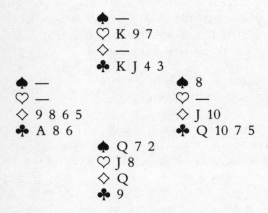

The declarer came to hand with a trump and Meckstroth had to watch while dummy's four clubs went away on three spades and a diamond.

So the challengers lost 14 IMPs on a deal where they seemed destined to gain 13. It was a blow from which they never recovered, though a similar swing did come their way later.

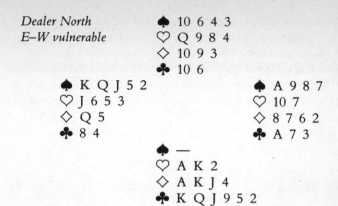

Dealer North
E–W vulnerable

North hand: ♠ 10 6 4 3 ♡ Q 9 8 4 ◇ 10 9 3 ♣ 10 6

West hand: ♠ K Q J 5 2 ♡ J 6 5 3 ◇ Q 5 ♣ 8 4

East hand: ♠ A 9 8 7 ♡ 10 7 ◇ 8 7 6 2 ♣ A 7 3

South hand: ♠ — ♡ A K 2 ◇ A K J 4 ♣ K Q J 9 5 2

The bidding was . . . peculiar:

South	West	North	East
Becker	Rosencranz	Rubin	Wold
—	—	1♠[1]	No
3NT[2]	No	4♠[3]	No
4NT[4]	No	5♣[5]	No
7♣[6]	No	7♠[7]	dble
7NT	No	No	dble
No	No	No	

[1] Even if your system contains various checks and balances, it seems silly, when you have a good lead in the match, to open with a psychic bid. However, Ira Rubin is not the type to break into an easy canter.

[2] He suspects that his partner has nothing and does not want to risk being left in any bid short of game.

[3] Becker had forgotten, but Rubin remembered, that the 3NT response signified a fair raise to game. He expects to be left in four spades.

[4] This was key-card Blackwood.

[5] Showing 0 or 3 key cards.

[6] Well, there was just room for three key cards.

[7] Did partner mean it? This was the first time clubs had been bid as a suit.

147

To lose 1100 in a freely bid grand slam is unusual even in family bridge.

I make no apology for describing these disasters. Competence may be praiseworthy, but it is the brilliancies and the howlers that inspire the oohs and aahs at any sport.

43

Enjoying an edge

Good players are always looking for ways to improve the odds in their favour. It is not a matter of minute calculations, more absorbing to mathematicians than to bridge players, but of discovering some extra possibility that can be exploited before, or in conjunction with, the main chance.

You will be annoyed with yourself if you don't see what was wrong with the declarer's play of the following hand:

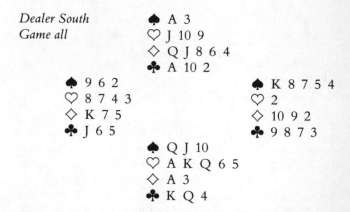

Dealer South
Game all

```
              ♠ A 3
              ♡ J 10 9
              ◇ Q J 8 6 4
              ♣ A 10 2
♠ 9 6 2                    ♠ K 8 7 5 4
♡ 8 7 4 3                  ♡ 2
◇ K 7 5                    ◇ 10 9 2
♣ J 6 5                    ♣ 9 8 7 3
              ♠ Q J 10
              ♡ A K Q 6 5
              ◇ A 3
              ♣ K Q 4
```

South opened 2NT and North, quite reasonably, raised to 6NT. West led a low heart and the declarer's first move was to play ace and another diamond. West played low, naturally, and the jack won. South took two more rounds of hearts, then finessed the queen of spades. So he went one down, looking rather foolish.

'The spade finesse was a better chance than to find the

diamonds 3–3,' South explained. 'Also, I make it if East has the king of spades but only two diamonds.'

This was true, but there was a better line of play. Instead of playing ace and another diamond, lead a low diamond from hand. If the queen wins, you can afford to lose a trick to the king of spades. If the diamond queen loses to the king, you can test the break in this suit before finessing in spades.

The point in the next example is a little more abstruse.

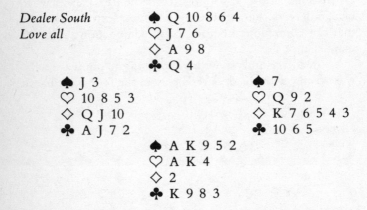

Dealer South
Love all

♠ Q 10 8 6 4
♡ J 7 6
♢ A 9 8
♣ Q 4

♠ J 3
♡ 10 8 5 3
♢ Q J 10
♣ A J 7 2

♠ 7
♡ Q 9 2
♢ K 7 6 5 4 3
♣ 10 6 5

♠ A K 9 5 2
♡ A K 4
♢ 2
♣ K 9 8 3

Again the bidding was brief: one spade – three spades – six spades. South won the diamond lead in dummy, drew two rounds of trumps, then led a low club to the queen, which held. A club return went to the 5, 9 and jack.

West exited with a diamond and South ruffed. With the K 8 of clubs left, he tried the 8 and had to ruff in dummy when West played low. There was no way to catch the queen of hearts, so a second trick was lost at the finish.

'Sorry, partner, I had to guess,' said South, not wishing to admit that he had been misled by East's amusing echo of the 6 and 5 of clubs. This had led him to suppose that the clubs were 3–4 and that the ace would fall on the third round.

'It seems to me that in any case you should have led the king of clubs on the third round,' said his partner. 'As the cards lie, you pin the 10. If this doesn't happen, you still have the chance of finding East with four clubs and the queen of hearts.'

South nodded sagely, but it is doubtful whether he appreciated the point. North meant: try the king of clubs on the third round; if it fails to pin the 10 you can play for this ending:

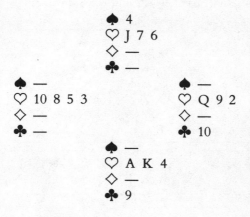

The lead is in dummy and the last trump squeezes East.

There is one other point you may have noticed on the way. Before tackling the clubs, declarer should eliminate the diamonds. Then, if West wins the second round of clubs he will be forced to open up the hearts, giving South an additional chance.

151

44

West complained, but it was his fault

Sometimes a defender can play his own game with no fear of being let down by his partner. Sometimes all that is needed is that partner should abstain from a foolish 'trance'.

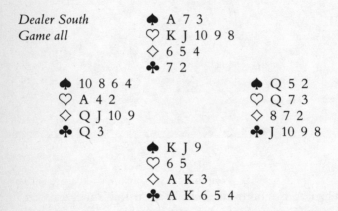

Dealer South
Game all

♠ A 7 3
♡ K J 10 9 8
◇ 6 5 4
♣ 7 2

♠ 10 8 6 4
♡ A 4 2
◇ Q J 10 9
♣ Q 3

♠ Q 5 2
♡ Q 7 3
◇ 8 7 2
♣ J 10 9 8

♠ K J 9
♡ 6 5
◇ A K 3
♣ A K 6 5 4

North–South reached the obvious 3NT and West led the queen of diamonds. South won the second round and led a heart to the jack. East, a good player, played low without any consideration.

South came back to the ace of clubs and led a second heart. This time he took a 'right view', going up with the king. When the suit split 3–3 he had ten tricks on top.

'Why didn't you take the queen of hearts?' asked West crossly.

'If I do, we only make two diamonds and two hearts, don't we?' East replied. 'There was a chance that declarer would finesse again in hearts. Then he can't establish the suit.'

West considered this point. Then he turned to South and asked, 'Why didn't you finesse again?'

'Because you obviously thought about going up with the ace on the second round,' South replied.

The defence on the next hand needed good timing by both defenders.

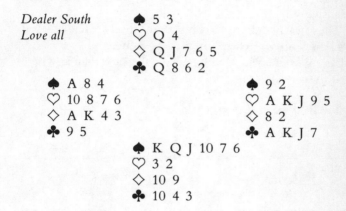

Dealer South
Love all

	♠ 5 3	
	♡ Q 4	
	◇ Q J 7 6 5	
	♣ Q 8 6 2	

♠ A 8 4		♠ 9 2
♡ 10 8 7 6		♡ A K J 9 5
◇ A K 4 3		◇ 8 2
♣ 9 5		♣ A K J 7

	♠ K Q J 10 7 6	
	♡ 3 2	
	◇ 10 9	
	♣ 10 4 3	

As North–South were not playing weak two bids, South had to choose between pass and three spades. He ventured three spades and the bidding continued:

South	West	North	East
3♠	No	No	dble[1]
No	No[2]	No	

[1] A difficult choice, but the double leaves open more possibilities than four hearts.

[2] A slam is possible, but in such situations, especially at rubber bridge, it is sensible to take the sure plus score.

West led the king of diamonds, noted his partner's 8,

and switched to a club. East cashed three tricks in clubs,
West discarding a heart, then played a diamond to the ace.
West returned a heart; East cashed two heart winners, then
led a fourth club. South ruffed high, while West discarded
a heart. Now the 10 of spades was taken by the ace, a
diamond was ruffed by the 9 of spades, and West's 8 x of
spades was promoted.

'Well, they could have made a slam,' said South
defensively.

'They nearly did,' replied North morosely. 'They scored
900, less your wretched honours, of course.'

East–West played well again on the next hand, where
South was declarer in 3NT.

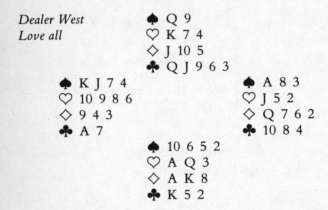

Dealer West
Love all

♠ Q 9
♡ K 7 4
♢ J 10 5
♣ Q J 9 6 3

♠ K J 7 4
♡ 10 9 8 6
♢ 9 4 3
♣ A 7

♠ A 8 3
♡ J 5 2
♢ Q 7 6 2
♣ 10 8 4

♠ 10 6 5 2
♡ A Q 3
♢ A K 8
♣ K 5 2

West, in the modern fashion, led the 9 of hearts (second
best from a weak suit), and South won with the ace. He led
a low club to the queen and a club back to the king and ace.

It was clear that the best chance for the defence lay in
spades. West made the excellent play of the king of spades,
East encouraged with the 8, and now the defenders took
four tricks in the suit. Note that if East has to attack this
suit, the 8 is the right card from his side.

154

45

Bidding for victory

Positional bidding is probably an unknown, certainly a misunderstood concept at 'the Vicarage'. In that setting it will be understood to refer to the major's penchant for playing the hand at any cost. At higher levels it can be a valuable scientific weapon.

```
Dealer North          ♠ Q 4
N–S vulnerable        ♡ K 6 4
                      ◇ A Q J 10 7
                      ♣ 8 4 3
   ♠ 6 3                            ♠ A J 10 9 8 7
   ♡ 9 8 7 3 2                      ♡ J 5
   ◇ 6 5                            ◇ K 3
   ♣ J 9 6 5                        ♣ Q 10 2
                      ♠ K 5 2
                      ♡ A Q 10
                      ◇ 9 8 4 2
                      ♣ A K 7
```

This is the amateur sequence:

South	West	North	East
—	—	1◇	1♠
3NT	No	No	No

A spade is led and, at best, South may make eight tricks with the aid of an end-play. (East has an awkward discard if South begins with three rounds of hearts.)

When you hold such as K x x or A x x of a suit bid on

your right, it may well be better for your partner, holding Q x or J x x, to become declarer. An expert pair might bid this hand as follows:

South	West	North	East
—	—	1◇	1♠
2♣[1]	No	2◇	No
2♠[2]	No	2NT	No
3NT	No	No	No

[1] South can always bid 3NT on a later round.
[2] This used to be called a 'directional asking bid'. The phrase has gone out of fashion, but the intention is clear: partner is asked to bid 2NT on a 'half-guard'. The system works well on this deal.

When your side has the balance of the cards you can afford to go slowly. On the next occasion I held the North cards. My partner bid rather well, played very poorly.

Dealer West
Game all

```
                    ♠ 4 3
                    ♡ A Q 10 9 7
                    ◇ A K J 9 7
                    ♣ 8
  ♠ A 5 2                         ♠ Q J 10 9 8 6
  ♡ 8 2                           ♡ 4 3
  ◇ Q 10 8 4 2                    ◇ —
  ♣ 4 3 2                         ♣ Q J 10 6 5
                    ♠ K 7
                    ♡ K J 6 5
                    ◇ 6 5 3
                    ♣ A K 9 7
```

South	West	North	East
—	No	1♡	1♠[1]
2♣[2]	2♠	3♢	4♢[3]
4♡	No	No	4♠
6NT[4]	No	No	No

[1] Many players, these days, would make a weak jump overcall, either two spades or three spades according to their methods.

[2] With a partner who has opened the bidding there is no need to leap.

[3] I suppose he hoped to give partner the lead in a heart contract and ruff the diamond return.

[4] This looks odd, but wasn't so silly. South judges that 6NT may be easier to make than six, or even five, hearts.

West began with a club to the 10 and ace. Obviously a deep finesse in diamonds wins twelve tricks easily, but South, having bid 6NT because he placed East with a void in diamonds, played two rounds of hearts and only then led a diamond. Realizing now that he lacked entries for two more diamond leads, he played the ace from dummy and had no chance after that.

This was tragic (for my side), because even after the bad start South can make the contract. If he keeps his nerve and finesses the 7 of diamonds (after a club lead, then ace and king of hearts), he can reach this ending:

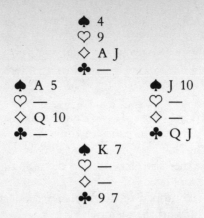

```
              ♠ 4
              ♡ 9
              ◇ A J
              ♣ —

♠ A 5                    ♠ J 10
♡ —                     ♡ —
◇ Q 10                  ◇ —
♣ —                     ♣ Q J

              ♠ K 7
              ♡ —
              ◇ —
              ♣ 9 7
```

Now the last heart from dummy kills West.

46

Best guess, no finesse

'I had to guess.' You have probably said this yourself on occasions, and certainly you have heard others say it. But if you study the matter closely, genuine guesses are very rare: there is almost always an indication one way or the other. Of course, no one can avoid taking wrong decisions; the best you can do in most cases is play with the odds. Two examples follow where one side or the other has to make a critical play.

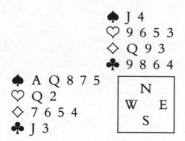

```
                        ♠ J 4
                        ♡ 9 6 5 3
                        ◇ Q 9 3
                        ♣ 9 8 6 4
        ♠ A Q 8 7 5      ┌─────────┐
        ♡ Q 2            │    N    │
        ◇ 7 6 5 4        │  W   E  │
        ♣ J 3            │    S    │
                        └─────────┘
```

South, who has a part score of 40, opens 2NT and all pass. Sitting West, you lead the 7 of spades. Dummy plays the jack, East the 2, and declarer the 3. The modern style is for defenders to show length in this type of position, so you place your partner with three spades.

At trick two the declarer leads a low heart from dummy; 4 from East, 8 from South, and you are in with the queen. What now? Most players would lead a diamond, but that's wrong. Why?

First, consider the heart situation. South probably has either A J 10 8 or A K 10 8; if A J 10 8, then he must certainly hold the top diamonds and the ace of clubs and you won't defeat the contract. It is better, therefore, to place him with A K 10 8. If at this point you can find partner with the ace of diamonds or the ace of clubs you will take six tricks. Which is more likely?

A slight misplay by the declarer has given you the best indication. His play of the 8 from the (presumed) holding of A K 10 8 in hearts shows that he was not concerned with keeping an entry to dummy. This surely means that he has the top diamonds. The full hand was:

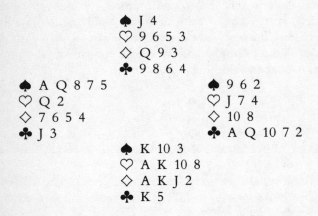

♠ J 4
♡ 9 6 5 3
◇ Q 9 3
♣ 9 8 6 4

♠ A Q 8 7 5   ♠ 9 6 2
♡ Q 2   ♡ J 7 4
◇ 7 6 5 4   ◇ 10 8
♣ J 3   ♣ A Q 10 7 2

♠ K 10 3
♡ A K 10 8
◇ A K J 2
♣ K 5

West switched to a diamond at the table and South made eight tricks. West spent the rest of the afternoon trying to work out hands where the diamond switch would be right, the club wrong.

I have no doubt that you will do better than the declarer on the next example:

Dealer West
Game all

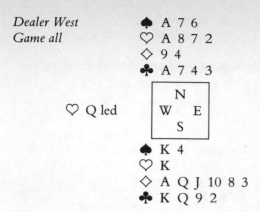

♠ A 7 6
♡ A 8 7 2
◇ 9 4
♣ A 7 4 3

♡ Q led

```
      N
  W       E
      S
```

♠ K 4
♡ K
◇ A Q J 10 8 3
♣ K Q 9 2

This time West opened four hearts as dealer and the bidding continued:

South	West	North	East
—	4♡	dble	No
4NT	No	5♣	No
7NT	No	No	No

North's five clubs showed 0 or 3 aces. South's 7NT showed that he was an optimist. 'I was down on the afternoon and I wanted to get square,' was his artless explanation.

West led the queen of hearts to South's king, East following suit. All followed low to the king of clubs and on the next round East discarded a spade. South played a third club to dummy's ace, then ran the 9 of diamonds. No good, for the full hand was:

161

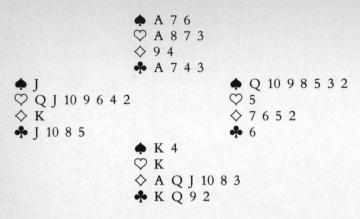

```
              ♠ A 7 6
              ♡ A 8 7 3
              ◇ 9 4
              ♣ A 7 4 3
♠ J                              ♠ Q 10 9 8 5 3 2
♡ Q J 10 9 6 4 2                 ♡ 5
◇ K                              ◇ 7 6 5 2
♣ J 10 8 5                       ♣ 6
              ♠ K 4
              ♡ K
              ◇ A Q J 10 8 3
              ♣ K Q 9 2
```

South was inconsolable when he found that the king of diamonds had been a singleton. 'I had 100 honours,' he remarked mournfully.

'They won't let you score them,' said his partner. 'You were in notrumps, remember, not in diamonds. When you found West with four clubs you knew eleven of his cards, seven hearts and four clubs. Cross to the ace of spades, and you know twelve. Now the *only* chance to bring in all the diamonds is to find West with a singleton king. Discard a club on the ace of hearts, then plonk down the ace of diamonds.'

47

Snick through the slips

At every big tournament you will see brilliant play interspersed with catastrophic blunders. Sometimes both will occur on the same deal.

In the match between Britain and Switzerland at Wiesbaden one year the Swiss declarer, Stanley Walter, found a bold and imaginative stroke to solve his problem. First I will show just the North and South hands.

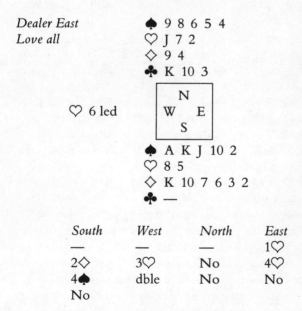

Dealer East
Love all

♠ 9 8 6 5 4
♡ J 7 2
◇ 9 4
♣ K 10 3

♡ 6 led

♠ A K J 10 2
♡ 8 5
◇ K 10 7 6 3 2
♣ —

South	West	North	East
—	—	—	1♡
2◇	3♡	No	4♡
4♠	dble	No	No
No			

A low heart was led. East cashed the ace and king, then led a low club to clarify the position in this suit. South ruffed with the 10 of spades. What do you suppose he did next?

If South cashes the ace and king of spades, then enters dummy with a low spade, he will be down to one trump and will surely run out of steam. Walter led a *low* spade and this was the full deal:

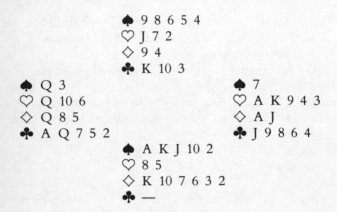

```
                ♠ 9 8 6 5 4
                ♡ J 7 2
                ◇ 9 4
                ♣ K 10 3
  ♠ Q 3                        ♠ 7
  ♡ Q 10 6                     ♡ A K 9 4 3
  ◇ Q 8 5                      ◇ A J
  ♣ A Q 7 5 2                  ♣ J 9 8 6 4
                ♠ A K J 10 2
                ♡ 8 5
                ◇ K 10 7 6 3 2
                ♣ —
```

West gave the 2 of spades half a look, then played low. After snicking this trick through the slips, declarer was home. He led a diamond to the king, cashed the ace of spades, and exited with a diamond. He was able to ruff the third diamond in dummy and make the rest.

In the other room Chris Duckworth, for Britain, also played in four spades doubled.

'I suppose you didn't think of leading a low spade from hand?' enquired the first West, his team-mate, at half-time.

'No, I can't say I did,' was the reply. 'You see, I was declarer from the North side. I don't think West would have played low if I had led the 2 of spades from dummy.'

There was another memorable hand in this tournament, played between Denmark and Turkey.

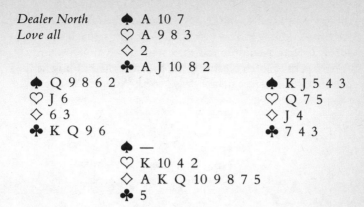

♠ A 10 7
♡ A 9 8 3
◇ 2
♣ A J 10 8 2

♠ Q 9 8 6 2
♡ J 6
◇ 6 3
♣ K Q 9 6

♠ K J 5 4 3
♡ Q 7 5
◇ J 4
♣ 7 4 3

♠ —
♡ K 10 4 2
◇ A K Q 10 9 8 7 5
♣ 5

Having discovered that his partner held an opening bid including three aces, Jens Auken, of Denmark, swiftly arrived in seven diamonds. He could, after all, count twelve top tricks.

But twelve tricks seemed to be all when West led the king of clubs. South won with the ace of clubs and played seven rounds of trumps, to arrive at this ending:

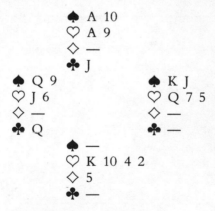

♠ A 10
♡ A 9
◇ —
♣ J

♠ Q 9
♡ J 6
◇ —
♣ Q

♠ K J
♡ Q 7 5
◇ —
♣ —

♠ —
♡ K 10 4 2
◇ 5
♣ —

On the last trump West made his best discard, a heart. South read the position well. He crossed to dummy with the ♡ A, cashed the ♠ A, and finessed the 10 of hearts for his thirteenth trick. It was a grand slam on a guard squeeze, surely a match-winning coup.

It won the match all right, for this was the bidding at the other table, where Turkey was North–South:

South	West	North	East
—	—	1♣	No
2♢	No	2♡	No
3♢	No	3♠	dble
redble	No	No	No

No doubt South's redouble, in the system, indicated first-round control of spades, but North had other ideas. Three spades redoubled was three down, a further 1000 to Denmark.

Denmark gained 20 IMPs and would have gained 14 even if Auken had gone one down in seven diamonds.

48

Banana skins for the brilliant

Do the experts search for opportunities to display their brilliance, or do they wait until the right hand appears? Yes, that is a searching question. The polite answer is that some experts are keener than others to see their name in lights.

This intended brilliance by one of Britain's leading pairs misfired badly.

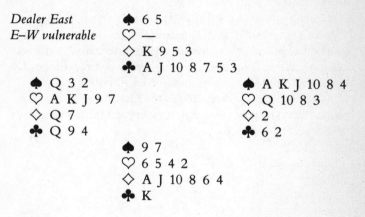

Dealer East
E–W vulnerable

North:
♠ 6 5
♡ —
♢ K 9 5 3
♣ A J 10 8 7 5 3

West:
♠ Q 3 2
♡ A K J 9 7
♢ Q 7
♣ Q 9 4

East:
♠ A K J 10 8 4
♡ Q 10 8 3
♢ 2
♣ 6 2

South:
♠ 9 7
♡ 6 5 4 2
♢ A J 10 8 6 4
♣ K

South	West	North	East
—	—	—	1♠
No	2♡	3♣	3♡
3NT[1]	4♡	No	No
4NT[2]	No	No[3]	dble
No	No	No	

[1] Meaning, I suppose, that he was prepared to sacrifice in either minor suit.

[2] Repeating the message; he knows, at least, that his partner must be short in hearts.

[3] He has concluded, apparently, that South has good values in the majors and passed over one spade because this was his best suit.

The defence had no difficulty in cashing six spades and five hearts to inflict a 1500 penalty. There may have been *some* sense in South's manoeuvres, and perhaps North was obtuse. When the enemy guns opened fire, obviously someone should have given the order to bale out.

My next example occurred in the Caribbean Championships. The fall guy this time was Steve Hamaoui, one of Venezuela's leading players.

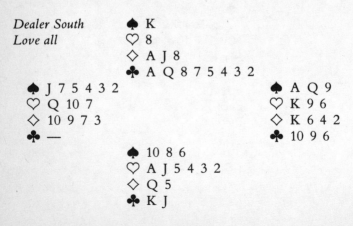

Dealer South
Love all

```
                    ♠ K
                    ♡ 8
                    ◇ A J 8
                    ♣ A Q 8 7 5 4 3 2
   ♠ J 7 5 4 3 2                      ♠ A Q 9
   ♡ Q 10 7                           ♡ K 9 6
   ◇ 10 9 7 3                         ◇ K 6 4 2
   ♣ —                                ♣ 10 9 6
                    ♠ 10 8 6
                    ♡ A J 5 4 3 2
                    ◇ Q 5
                    ♣ K J
```

Hamaoui (East) heard his opponents bid as follows:

South	West	North	East
1♥	No	2♣	No
2♥	No	3♦	No
3NT	No	No	No

West led the 2 of spades, the low card indicating that the player could see no chance of establishing a defence in any other suit. Hamaoui won with the ace and thought (very reasonably) (a) that South must have at least J x x in spades, and (b) that if South held a singleton king of clubs it might be vital to knock out dummy's entry, the ace of diamonds. So he tried a low diamond at trick two and the declarer made eleven tricks.

Another example of a brilliant play that was unlucky to fail occurred during a match between France and Italy in the annual 'Tournament of Champions' at Deauville.

Dealer North
E–W vulnerable

	♠ A K 8 7 6 5
	♥ A
	♦ 5 4
	♣ J 9 6 5

♠ Q J 4	♠ 10 3
♥ J 9	♥ Q 10 8 7 6 5 3 2
♦ J 3	♦ 10 2
♣ Q 10 8 7 4 2	♣ K

♠ 9 2
♥ K 4
♦ A K Q 9 8 7 6
♣ A 3

The French pair, Stetten and Faigenbaum, played in seven diamonds. Clubs had not been mentioned, but North had made a cue-bid in hearts. This induced Garozzo, West, to make the fine lead of a heart: he judged that South would be ruffing a spade and would need the ace of hearts as an entry.

The diagnosis was perfect – but the patient died, because South had twelve tricks on top and West was squeezed in spades and clubs. The only consolation – a small one, since the grand slam was not bid at the other table – was that the contract could not have been defeated.

49

'Well, I didn't . . .'

There was a player at Lederer's Club in the early days, Phyllis Titmas, who gave rise to a phrase that was still current when I made my appearance at the bridge clubs in the early 1950s. It was her habit to present one of the good players with a hand of approximately thirteen cards and begin on these lines:

'My partner opened one spade, the next player bid two diamonds, we were vulnerable, and this was my hand. What would you have bid?'

After the hand has been amended you suggest, say, two hearts, which seems fairly obvious. Phyllis goes on:

'Well, I didn't. I bid such-and-such, partner rebid four spades, what would you have done now?'

You say 'Pass', and Phyllis goes on:

'Well, I didn't. I bid 4NT and . . .'

I was reminded of this character when a friend, Alfred Huberman, showed me this hand:

♠ A J 10 9 8 4
♡ A Q 10 8 7 2
♢ 4
♣ —

'You are South and the bidding goes:

South	West	North	East
—	No	No	3NT
4♠	5♢	No	5NT
?			

'What do you say now?'

Alfred, I knew, had been a fearless rear-gunner during the last war. Not wanting to seem to be lacking in initiative, I suggested six hearts. One reason was that the lead against 5NT might be critical. In six hearts I would be exposed to less flak.

Alfred showed me the full hand:

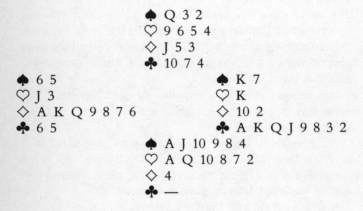

♠ Q 3 2
♡ 9 6 5 4
◇ J 5 3
♣ 10 7 4

♠ 6 5
♡ J 3
◇ A K Q 9 8 7 6
♣ 6 5

♠ K 7
♡ K
◇ 10 2
♣ A K Q J 9 8 3 2

♠ A J 10 9 8 4
♡ A Q 10 8 7 2
◇ 4
♣ —

'Well, I didn't,' he said, unconsciously reviving the famous phrase. 'I doubled, East stood it, and we collected 1900, as I led the ace of hearts. Still,' he added kindly, 'you do all right in six hearts. Not so good if partner puts you back to spades.'

Feeling that I had some ground to make up, I tested Alfred on a remarkable hand from rubber bridge. You hold as West:

♠ J 6 5
♡ 8 7 4
◇ A K J 7 3
♣ 4 2

The bidding follows this unusual course:

South	West	North	East
—	—	—	No
7♣	No	No	dble
redble	No	No	No

'What do you lead?' I asked him.

'A heart. What happened?'

'Why a heart?' I asked grimly.

'Obviously South is void of diamonds and partner has doubled because he can ruff a major suit. Isn't South more likely to hold a side suit of hearts than spades, since you have the jack of spades?'

Yes, and this was the full hand:

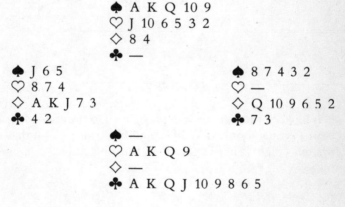

'I did manage to find the heart lead,' I remarked.

'You were lucky that North didn't transfer to seven hearts,' Alfred scoffed. He likes to have the last word.

50

Tales of mystery and imagination

How does this problem strike you? The contract is six clubs and West leads the queen of spades.

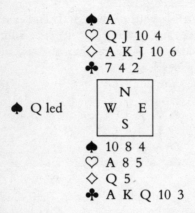

♠ A
♡ Q J 10 4
♢ A K J 10 6
♣ 7 4 2

♠ Q led

N
W E
S

♠ 10 8 4
♡ A 8 5
♢ Q 5
♣ A K Q 10 3

It looks as though you can play a club to the ace and will have a problem only if West has all five trumps. But that's not quite right. Suppose East has the long clubs:

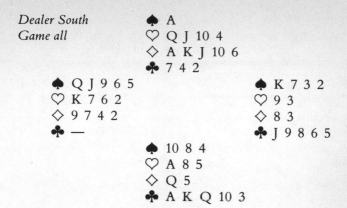

Dealer South
Game all

```
                    ♠ A
                    ♡ Q J 10 4
                    ♢ A K J 10 6
                    ♣ 7 4 2
♠ Q J 9 6 5                           ♠ K 7 3 2
♡ K 7 6 2                             ♡ 9 3
♢ 9 7 4 2                             ♢ 8 3
♣ —                                   ♣ J 9 8 6 5
                    ♠ 10 8 4
                    ♡ A 8 5
                    ♢ Q 5
                    ♣ A K Q 10 3
```

You may think that when East follows suit you should insert the 10 of clubs. That's not quite good enough. You may ruff a spade and play on diamonds, but East is going to ruff and you will be cut off from the dummy.

Another possibility is to win with the ace of clubs, intending to return a low one, but this doesn't produce enough tricks either, because East will return a third club.

Well, it's not so difficult if you are used to solving problems. The super-safe play is to duck the first round of clubs completely, letting East's 5 hold the trick. The best he can do is return a trump, but you will have enough tricks – four clubs, five diamonds, one heart, one spade and one ruff.

The interesting part about all this is that when a distinguished Hungarian died recently, a compatriot attributed this play to him in a piece for the IBPA Bulletin. At rubber bridge. In 1934!

Sometimes one feels not that the story is invented but that there may be a *slight* exaggeration in the way the diagram is constructed. The following story, from a match between Bermuda and Canada in the qualifying round of the Bermuda Bowl, has appeared in several magazines:

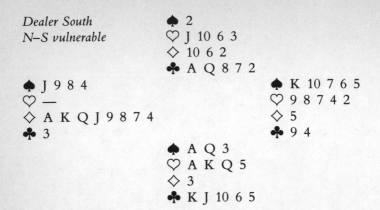

Dealer South
N–S vulnerable

	♠ 2	
	♡ J 10 6 3	
	◇ 10 6 2	
	♣ A Q 8 7 2	
♠ J 9 8 4		♠ K 10 7 6 5
♡ —		♡ 9 8 7 4 2
◇ A K Q J 9 8 7 4		◇ 5
♣ 3		♣ 9 4
	♠ A Q 3	
	♡ A K Q 5	
	◇ 3	
	♣ K J 10 6 5	

When Bermuda was North–South the bidding went:

South	West	North	East
1♣[1]	5♣[2]	dble	5◇[3]
6♣[4]	No	No	No

[1] Conventional.
[2] A transfer to diamonds.
[3] Well judged, since it may be better for the unknown hand to become declarer.
[4] However, South takes a bold and good decision.

Just one glance is enough to know what happened. West (it is said) led the 4 of diamonds and South played *low* from dummy; East won with the 5 and gave his partner the ruff.

Well, perhaps it happened just like that; but not every frog you kiss will turn into a prince.